Influencing the Collective Unconscious Mind

By   Nick Sambrook

Copyright © 2023 Nick Sambrook. All rights reserved.

Published May 2023

ISBN/SKU: 978-0-9928898-9-0

The right of Nick Sambrook to be identified as the author has been asserted by him in accordance with the Copyright and Patents Act 1988

All rights reserved. With the exception of excerpts for preview and sharing purposes, this book may not be reproduced or transmitted in any form or by any means, electronic or mechanical, including photocopying, recording, or by any information storage or retrieval system.

www.nicksambrook.com
nicksambrook@outlook.com

First Edition

Awakening to the knowledge, experience, and understanding that a collective unconscious mind of humanity exists...

... is one thing

Knowing that we are all interconnected as part of a trans-human consciousness and experiencing that yourself ...is another

.. but doing something about it, and being able to influence it, do something about it and change things...

.. is a whole new, and much harder ballgame.

It's the difference between being a spectator or a commentator on the events ...

...to having 'skin in the game'.

REFACE

Attempting to describe many of these concepts in this book is a very hard thing to do. Even knowing where to start is somewhat difficult without appreciating what the reader has as a reference point, or level of scientific understanding, awareness or experience of the 'non-physical' and/or any preconceived religious or spiritual ideas.

Many of these newer ideas or concepts are also hard for people to understand and identify with and relate to, unless they have experienced some extreme non-physical event such as an out of body experience, a vision, vivid dreams, ghosts, 'aliens', religious 'awakening', or had a near death experience.

Yet even with these experiences your interpretation and understanding and belief may be overly influenced by existing cultural pre-programming and perception. This 'spiritual position' experience and vivid exposure to the 'pleroma' will be formed and perceived with a physical worldview interpretation or translation, and not necessarily just by you. Others in the past who have applied real physical world interpretations to the virtual-datascape and in so doing reinforcing them and giving them shape and form.

Sometimes it is better to start from the atheistic position and stance, and then work backwards, relying on science, logic, evidence, with a sceptical 'not easily fooled' attitude.

Hopefully by the end of this book you will have more of an understanding that all of these experiences and spiritual and religious models originate and are sourced by the same 'thing' (just with different individual cognitive interpretations or perceptions). In essence all these types of experience and interpretation are all simply originating from the same (programmable) information field structure. It is just that our interpretations are shaped and influenced by historical interpretations, archetypal patterning, physical perception, and naïve beliefs. Yet all come from the same domain.

This book attempts to articulate and describe as best as possible in simplified terms the *form* and *nature* of the entity of our collective mind (not just a shared transpersonal virtual data landscape of an interconnected humanity, but as a collective entity in its own right). Something that we (humanity) have naturally evolved and developed for and by ourselves, and yet by collective natural evolutionary processes we have necessarily become blind to, and yet ultimately controlled by as a species of cultures.

This 'entity' that is 'us' (let us use the term 'IT' thus avoiding other overused terms and concepts), is part of both the physical world (from which it is generated or engrammed), and an integrated counterpart element in the programmable field-based information 'spiritual' Pleroma system (or the etheric non-physical sub-quantum field structure – or the 'spiritual' 'other side', or even '5th Dimension' for want of better adjectives. All of which operates together as an integrated dual paradigm of consciousness, a physical and non-physical combined system – which we have created like a virtual landscape, and world built upon a pre-existing 'operating system'.

This book also provides some of the answers readers have been looking for in a more scientific form, and describes concepts that are by their nature very hard to articulate in physical 'real world' terminology. Most of the concepts exist within a different paradigm from that we have become accustomed to in our physical word perception and understanding of.

3 Influencing the Collective Unconscious Mind

It is not easy to describe what something is 'like' when it is nothing like anything at all. Explaining the phenomena is like having a clear series of pictures of a complete unified concept of everything downloaded into your mind but being unable to find the words to describe it all together, and being limited by language, tenure, analogy, and scope of comparison. Without also being drawn down existing rabbit holes of belief structures.

It is also (more importantly) trying to provide some ideas (including ones identified by others) on how this collective unconscious can be influenced, changed, and/or evolved.

These ideas have been consolidated from many thousands of pages of exegesis notes, ideas, gnosis downloads, evidence, study observations, (and navigation through volumes of philosophical, scientific, and esoteric study) to provide a more synthesized holistic overview.

The book also focuses on techniques on how you can influence this collective mind yourself, and what evidence and effects to look out for and how this can manifest itself in the physical 'real world'.

Once you understand that our everyday consciousness is in essence at the juncture or combination of two realities. The external world of the physical that we perceive and 'know', and the internal esoteric world described in myth, religion, spiritual, or the collective trans-personal imaginal. Then you can change it, rather than just being oblivious to it.

This collective human 'Overmind' is after all programmable – we have been doing it for millions of years, yet together—now with conscious thoughts and intention— we can influence ITs direction. Rather than blindly continuing along unconscious rhythmical pathways which have all worked well until now.

If IT is us and we are IT ..

(that is our Collective Unconscious Overmind)

... then we can change IT.

Hopefully by doing so it will also create a better picture of what we are dealing with, why we are here, what we need to do, and what needs to change.

After all we can no longer allow existing dogmatic controlling governing systems and blind mythological political and individual habitual processes to dictate our future in its inevitable course towards the iceberg.

ACKNOWLEDGMENTS

With thanks to Prof Stephen Schafer for his encouragement in getting these ideas into coherent form.

Thanks also to Prof Alex Bennet for her support, help, and the *Myst* images for the book cover etc

Thankyou also to my daughter Charlie Sambrook
for the amazing work on the book cover design
and especially for my wife
Jan
for her love, support, and for being a true angel.

Table of Contents

PREFACE | 1
ACKNOWLEDGMENTS | 4
FOREWARD by Prof Stephen Brock Schafer | 7

Chapter 1: What is the Collective Unconscious Mind | 13
Chapter 2: In a Virtual war with ourselves | 29
Chapter 3: How IT Changes and Evolves Through Us | 34
Chapter 4: The Form of IT and Communication with IT | 43
Chapter 5: The Evolution of IT | 52
Chapter 6: Immunisation and Control Games | 56
Chapter 7: Perceiving IT in Different Ways | 59
Chapter 8: The Legacy Issues of Our Collective Mind | 71
Chapter 9: We Can't See the Woods for the Trees | 76
Chapter 10: Structure and Form of the Collective Mind | 85
Chapter 11: What is IT Influenced By? | 90
Chapter 12: The Way Forward | 97
Chapter 13: How to Influence 'IT' | 100
Chapter 14: Blueprint for Humanity | 120
Chapter 15: How to Measure the Change | 124
Chapter 16: What can be achieved | 127
Chapter 17: Endnote with Fictional Excerpt | 128

ADDITIONAL READING LIST | 135

Foreward

Comments by Prof Stephen Brock Schafer

Scientific-philosophical discussion of such issues related to *Pleroma* or the totality of divine powers are endless, but it is rare to contemplate the collective unconscious/conscious as a human collective *Overmind* in and of itself.

A sentient macro entity existing in its own right, and existential as a combined collective mind and physical humanity. It is even more rare to suggest that such an *entity*—what the author calls 'IT'—has not evolved properly (mainly due to lack of natural external competition). As such is in need of re-programming and evolving beyond legacy traits, and habits.

This book is not an *orthodox* academic/scientific treatment of ontological dimensions of the paranormal. Instead, meaningful insights addressed in the book are based on the unique personal extreme experiences of the author, (and of others), combined with extensive scientific and esoteric study.

In order to represent the authority and authenticity of the author's uniquely valuable paranormal and surreal physical experiences and evidence, it is critical to provide some biographical insight. Thirty years ago, the author left academia with degrees in Cybernetics and Computer Science and post graduate qualifications that led to owning and managing several Information Communication Technology companies. Becoming an expert on secure ICT systems development, he went on to manage many international systems technology projects, provided business change consultancy for many large international organisations.

Since the age of five his life has also followed an imposed experimental structure provided by Joseph Campbell's *Hero Journey*[1] which is based on Carl Jung's psychological dynamic of *individuation and transcendence*. These stages of the journey are symbolically represented in the Jungian dreamscape which is understood to incorporate both the individual (personal) and collective unconscious agendas.

In esoteric terms employed by the world's Mystery Schools, many humans incarnate within the fractal structure of the hero journey. Therefore, the author's unusual experiences may be contemplated within this established context that has both an esoteric *spiritual* basis and a physical basis. As such from an early age, the author also experienced being directed by some sort of external collective unconscious childlike mentality that was somehow outside of his own authority or psyche. By the age of eight he had outgrown any spiritual beliefs, and was a sceptical atheist. Despite this, in March 2005 he had a twenty-minute-long extreme cosmic (consciousness) paranormal experience characterized by overwhelming gnosis that is narrated in the first chapter of his fictional partial autobiography—*IT: Pieces in the Dark* (2014). An experience he was able to treat objectively and scientifically.

Since that initiation into a Gnostic state-of-being, that state has persisted. In other words, the author has been conscripted into an ongoing evolving experience of gnosis and esoteric interaction. Specifically, the experience has been conducive to insights relative to the importance of synchronicities for dealing with a Gnostic reality of *spontaneity* in which the global media-field becomes a collective—often mediated—Jungian dreamscape and knowledgebase. He has also worked and experimented with

---

[1] Campbell, J. (1950). *The hero with a thousand faces.* New World Library.

some of the most experienced international healers—leading-edge spiritual minded people—spiritualists, channelers, and experts on paranormal esotericism. All in-order to gain insights and understanding, not just providing a scientific academic compartmentalised narrow perspective.

As mentioned above, in conjunction with his *paranormal* work, the author has also worked with (and sponsored) some of the leading scientific authorities in an unprecedented attempt to bring together all perspectives into one synthesized concept without condescending to academic departmentalized-compartmentalized attitudes and scholarly opinions, or religious dogma.

The author has also combined the knowledge he has gained from these peak experiences with extensive study in the field of consciousness, philosophy, depth psychology, mythology and quantum mechanics, all of which he is able to process and comprehend surprisingly easily despite having no previous academic tenure in these areas.

As a starting point for reading this book it would be an advantage to the reader to have studied the work Carl Jung (including *The Red Book* and *Answer to Job*) and some of the authors who have studied Jung's work such as J. Jacobi and Peter Kingsley[2]. In addition to Jung, some synthesis of postmodern philosophy, cultural forms of collective discourse, and theories of consciousness are recommended.

With many authors and academics there is a tendency to be circumspect, hinting or suggesting what is going on, speculating about related theories rather than being specific, whilst still attempting to build on others work. Refreshingly, in this book the author attempts—from a broad perspective

---

[2] Kingsley, Peter (2018). Catafalque: Carl Jung and the end of humanity. (2004). Reality. (2010). A story waiting to pierce you.

to describe what 'IT' is, what is going on, why, and what needs to be done about 'IT', and how.

The author has also researched extensively the dozen or so quantum unified field *theories of everything* and found that although some have elements to them that are logical, none of them are fully correct. Some have large logical problems or only partly describe the mind numbingly complex field-based information system (*consciousness*) for which we still only have a limited physical worldview paradigm interpretation (and of which the physical universe is only a perceived subset).

All the theories are either mathematical (which is a language not a solution), scientific, or philosophical models, all trying to reach out from a limited physical worldview perspective, attempting to conceptualize and rationalize something that doesn't make sense from this physical direction, and for which we have limited evidential perspective and understanding, and which doesn't take account of the esoteric evidence.

The ontological position that should be taken is to first determine what sort of unified system needs to be in place to *create* the physical universe *from*—rather than the other way around—and then form a model/picture of that using logic, analogy, information models, scientific and esoteric (spiritual) evidence, and practical experimental experience.

Many of these theories of everything are simply generated from ideas to explain away illogical weird quantum effects and strange anomalies in the physical universe, abstractions within a perceived interpreted physical reality from an alternate paradigm but with a limited worldview imagination (i.e., guesses).

For example, the concept of *infinite universes* is only there as a solution to attempt to make sense of perplexing quantum phenomena that are projected into reality.

However, just because gamers are enmeshed in a Final Fantasy computer game with infinite permutations and perceptual pixels doesn't mean there are an infinite number of operating systems running it.

The various theories of consciousness are similarly inadequate because they are far too limited to the brain as opposed to the mind. The theories seem, for the most part, coming from the wrong direction (i.e., physical to etheric) rather than explaining how the physical universe can be created and consciously perceived through and <u>from</u> a unified field-set of integrated consciousness, which is the greater part of an overall field-based information system of which physical reality is a subset and lesser (yet key paradigm) part.

For decades, theories of consciousness took the wrong direction. Few scholars took a pantheistic approach to science, and perspectives from quantum field theory didn't really take hold until research by Hameroff and Penrose[3] discovered sentience in neural microtubules. More recent works such as with Meijer and Bruek[4] address a much more holistic and combined rational theory to both consciousness and a unified quantum field theory. There are also new developments in the approach of computation universal field theories.

In this book the author prefers the use of information communication systems analogies to describe elements of,

---

[3] Hameroff, S., & Penrose, R. (2014). Consciousness in the universe: A review of the 'Orch OR' theory. *Physics of Life Reviews 11*, 39-78.
[4] Meijer, D. K. F., with Bruek, R. L. (2020*). A new premise for quantum physics, consciousness and the fabric of reality.* Researchgate.net.

and the nature of, the collective unconscious, and the *persona* of the collective entity of humanity – which he describes as 'IT'.

He finds that the only way to describe this field-based information system structure (architecture, data flows and workings) of 'IT' is by using technology metaphors and analogies, which have been created in the real world of technology for the very purpose of emulating (simulating) this preternatural *elephant in the room*....

In other words, this little book is a sort of practical *field guide* for groups or individuals to give some perspective on what we are dealing with here, rather than just relying solely on leading-edge, academic, self-supporting, departmentally organised constructs such as papers and books. All of which have built up ever higher, and ever more defensively, over the last several decades.

Expanding on that work, this book is designed for those who (rather than being constrained by orthodox procedure) want to come out of the safety of their ivory towers and create coordinated coherent change and do something exciting and productive …

….rather than just talking about it.

Chapter 1

WHAT IS THE COLLECTIVE UNCONCIOUS MIND

So Imagine for a moment that we really *are* living in the world in the Matrix films (created by the Wachowskis from various post-modern philosophical ideas and theories, e.g., by Jean Baudrillard)[5] and that this physical world you perceive as REAL *is* a virtual reality 3D projection translated into your mind by your senses – which science now tells us is the case – a worldview dreamscape that is shared by everyone in which we all act out various characters in an ongoing role-playing game and screenplay script. A reality governed by time, rules, dimensional constraints and laws.

Reality as such, is a combination of physical 'reality' that we can perceive and have created a perception of - in our minds - and fed by a collective imaginal virtual scape of data underlying it.

But, unlike in the films, there are no machines controlling us or computers generating this virtual reality perception from some other physical world version. Yet, you exist both here in the physical world, and also in another paradigm virtual world that supports the perception of our individual and collective consciousness. A sort of physical Role Playing Game (RPG) world and an operating system in some virtual server that runs it, and is projecting it into physical reality..

Physical reality perception, after all, is something we have created in our minds to make sense of something that doesn't. Our minds interpret what we see into forms.

---

[5] Baudrillard, J. (1982). Simulacra and simulation.

The problem, though, is how to describe what exists and what is happening on the 'other side of the mirror', the 'down the rabbit hole' realm or domain. A domain where information is held, projected, and supports and integrates with our perceived physical world.

Well, that's the tricky part, and where the difficulty is. Trying to describe and express this paradoxical domain using analogies can only go so far; it is difficult to describe something that is indescribable in physical real-world terms, and from which we have so little physical and scientific evidence. So, this Matrix world idea is just a starting point to try to create a shared platform.

It is also hard to create an analogy or context when there is no time or dimensionality in this 'spiritual' domain, this Pleroma, this information field-based quantum system that projects information into our physical reality at every point and on many levels and hierarchy. Life-informing data seemingly emanating from nowhere.

In addition to life formation and nature evolving data, this matrix of information on the 'other side' is also full of human-developed libraries of knowledge – landscapes of dreams – legend domains – a mass of interwoven imagination worldscapes. Data that we have created and built ourselves over many millennia from and within the physical laws, constraints, and naturally-evolved storylines, all contained within and supported by a pre-existing global information quantum field operating system and server. Like some vast self-regulating evolving AI system built on and refined with myth, media, archetypal functions, natural laws and constraints, traits, needs, controls, and self-preservation influences and beliefs.

This quantum field-based information system supports the individual by creating them with a programmed blueprint from a set of templates, an archetypal and cultural set of building blocks which themselves have slowly refined over millennia from previously developed – naturally evolving – building blocks.

Yet, there is a controlled bandwidth of information flow and energy between the two paradigms at the lowest (quantum) levels. Also, only a very small proportion of this alternate paradigm is projected into physicality. Conversely, this information structure can be interactively programmed through conscious life forms in a limited and controlled way.

So, within this alternate domain we have a coexistence with our individual physical body and mind (like some sort of physical device and software interacting with a cloud version). With data and history stored in a different way to how information is stored physically.

The same is also the case for all of humanity as a collective entity which is and of itself alive, limited only by the rules and constraints of the world sphere server in which it has grown from and within. It is otherwise self regulating and adaptive, evolving its own existence, its own bodily (hive or colony type) development (which is all held as part of us), unconscious thought and higher level programs , macro intelligence and knowledge - all over and above that which has been developed by and from the individuals that have created it through different cultures and civilisations through natural selection.

As individuals and society in general become more intelligent and complex this entity has had to naturally develop more sophisticated methods and techniques for controlling, containing, directing and hypnotising those individuals and groups.

Attempting to describe this 'Matrix' though is what highly intelligent scientists, nuclear physicists, biologists, philosophers, mathematicians, etc have desperately been trying (driven) to do – and to explain, demonstrate and 'get to' - for many decades now.

These 'Theories of Everything' or 'Unified Field Theories', along with philosophical models, and theories of consciousness.

The main problem being that the very thing we are trying to describe is evolving. It is like being in Plato's cave which has now evolved to become a physical high definition virtual 3D reality version where the film projection originates from everywhere, formed and generated by a quantum information system interface - in which our consciousness's cohabit and evolve in an alternate paradigm.

Many others have focused on specific aspects of the whole thing such as well-meaning New Age psychonauts, spiritualists, prophets and shaman, as well as religious academics, and truth seekers. All of whom have their own objective views, experiences, rabbit holes, agendas, and worldview interpretative perceptions of the 'other side of the mirror' yet all being driven to express what it is they are experiencing. These are views orientated and dependent on which part of the 'elephant in the room' they are connected to or interested in. All perceiving parts of the same thing.

It is very difficult for anyone to describe the whole thing in some form of logical picture or even to know where to start. What is required is a more overall or holistic picture and a synthesis between the scientific and spiritual (experiential) objective views.

And I am no different in that respect, other than of course having the physical evidence and extreme experiences. Still though I will try and provide a very logical and scientific and evidential picture from many sides.

However, I should also point out that you probably won't like what I have to say.

So, in this book I am not going to go into complex universal field theories of everything or philosophical debates on existence and consciousness – I am simply going to concentrate on us (humanity) and how we exist within this alternate dual paradigm both individually and as a collective entity – IT (a generic term I have used to avoid any religious associations, and as an acronym for what I believe describes it's information system form and nature).

So elaborating on the Morpheus quote in the first Matrix film "…there's something wrong with the world. You don't know what it is, but it's there…..

….Do you want to know what it is?"

… well here goes…

So 'IT' (from my experiences and study) is the entity of our collective human unconscious mass mind, over and beyond the trans-human Jungian collective unconscious experienced by so many individuals, and which has evolved over many millennia.

It is a highly complex and sophisticated integrated collective *'hive-type'* Overmind and physical 'humanity' body, a co-evolving biological program structured, field-based operating/information hologrammatic system. This is supported within a Gaian (nature) quantum information field 'operating system' and global knowledge field. Which in turn is supported by a quantum field based planetary global 'server' and physical world device (solid state information processing machine or 'philosopher's stone').

It's ok I know the previous paragraphs are a bit complex so just keep reading. I will try and explain it in several ways.

In IT we (as individual humans) are component interworking informational and physical devices (as cells within a macro-organism) containing and running programs which operate within us, both as individuals, and on behalf of this meta-organism information knowledge database of civilization/cultural structure. All supporting a consciousness of a shared and negotiated exo-memory, or distributed networked knowledge data, and programmable operating system, which is our 'god' that we are creating and evolving. IT has evolving cosmic 'sentience' (awareness) that has advanced far beyond its original prehistoric egg-state.

As I have experienced it, 'IT' is a Karmic 'spiritual' creature of our own making, not something 'other' or some external entity. We (humanity) have created and evolved this collective *Overmind* or entity ourselves (a common OneMind as referred to by Larry Dossey[6]) over many millennia, and it is architecturally formed of (and by) evolving cultures.

IT contains all our knowledge and programs within this field based information system (including psyche structures) from base level subconscious strata to higher levels (built up through ever higher, peer-to-peer information systems communication models) evolving between the physical and the etheric non-physical as a shared and jointly negotiated path.

This collective consciousness entity is what we have evolved from natural evolutionary drives/needs/selection and physical rules, and then reinforced and adapted and grown in awareness and level of consciousness in parallel to ourselves as individuals. We are, in effect, all fractal hologram perceptions of a kaleidoscopically potentially infinite 'one

---

[6] Dossey, L. (2013). *One mind.* Hay House Publishing.

mind'. This one mind of humanity is far more sophisticated and complex and hierarchical than Jung's concept of the collective unconscious with its archetypes and forms, derived mostly through intuitive collation of extreme individual esoteric experiences, including Jung's own extreme experiences (as also described in his Red Book).

So, whereas Carl Jung's concept of the trans-human collective unconscious exists, he really only touched on aspects that were observable (and related) to individuals i.e. the archetypal building blocks and functions that made up individuals. Ones that could be perceived and determined through psychoanalysis.

There are layers of macro programming, functionality, and intercommunication also going on at a cultural and human civilization level, too. Forming a giant AI- like system that we as individuals are hidden from and unaware of. So again, if you imagine the Matrix film combined with the Truman show and Free Guy and the worst most unbelievable trashy depressing soap opera, you can find - and you will not be far from the screenplay reality we have scripted for ourselves, and are enslaving ourselves within.

As the saying goes … 'If the devil didn't exist man would probably have created one'. Well that's exactly what we did do, and the same can be said for all forms of perceived or interpreted deities.

IT can only be expressed effectively in analogy form, for we do not have the words to describe IT. Nothing in the physical world can describe this 'zeitgeist' in terms of shape, nature, dynamics, hierarchy, function, and complexity, or the quantum field-based information structure framework IT exists in.

IT can potentially only be accurately analogized as a metaphor using complex information systems architectures, models, data terminology, and ICT analogy akin to quantum computer architecture in concept and nature.

Which is why so many people have historically found it impossible to describe from their experiences of it, and yet still manage to build elaborate yet naïve religions around.

People historically have attempted to articulate or describe aspects of it through art, poetry, film, philosophy, science, and so forth. A form of cultural discourse trying to express and articulate that which they have experienced or feel or want to express, within them, and through them.

However, this work can only describe parts or component elements or interpretive expressions of IT. Equally people adopt or interpret previously perceived ideas, and are inclined to use existing models of belief structures (particularly religious models) to relate to it, and give it architecture, hierarchy. Yet all, in essence, perceptions with differing interpretations of the same thing.

They may also perceive and recognize it through translating symbolisms or whatever has come into their sphere of consciousness in the past, and then follow the well-trodden path down that particular rabbit hole.

This is in effect a form of hypnotic, naïve, self-reinforcing interpretation combined with personal background, culture, knowledge and surroundings that pre-programs or pre-cognizes interpretation of spiritual experiences into existing religious dogmatic interpretations. In effect re-visioning others previously interpreted perceptions and creative ideas. All combined with physical world perception of objects, laws, rules, story and nature.

However, there are no existing naïve belief structures (religions) that come anywhere close to truly defining or describing its complexity, or its logical scientific definition.

Influencing the Collective Unconscious Mind

All the religions seem to be derived from previous individual extreme spiritual experiences with IT as it evolves (building on each other and evolving dynamically).

Each new theory and philosophy of everything building and moving on from previous ones. Until they eventually become outdated or unable to adaptively evolve. Even now, moving from quantum physics unified field theories to a more computational unified theory of everything (or CUTE).

As such we have built a technological media-field (dream-like media-sphere) which appears to be embedded with preternaturally-induced dynamics that afford collective humanity an opportunity for recognizing its historical incoherent influences. We now have the opportunity to refine it along coherently entrained frequencies of intention in a conscious (deliberate) rather than unconscious (blind religious) fashion.

We have become a computer-like and computer-dependent society in emulation of what is happening on the other side of the mirror. As such both sides are ever more simulating and reinforcing each other but with no clear conscious direction or purpose.

The overall problem is that our humanity collective '*Overmind/Supermind*' entity (IT) has not evolved properly – mainly due to a lack of natural external competition and naïve understanding – and now it is in need of conscious reprogramming intervention.

As an analogy, we are ants in the colony of this hive-style 'god' mind (a giant ant computer and information storage), a collective human entity that has become so controlling, adaptive, devious, manipulative and hidden that we are unconsciously blind to it as individuals, and unaware how much it controls us.

We live within IT and are hypnotically unaware of how it influences us, our cultural environments and civilizational ebbs and flows. IT affects how society is structured, politics, governmental control structures, crowd mentality, compartmentalized academia, and stovepipe insular narrow scientific delusional mind-sets.

Yet we are the ones who have created and evolved IT and shaped it, made it what it is, a collective bubble

Especially those 'hero' archetypes (programs in individuals) whose natural biological purpose is to refine it, evolve it, give it ideas, all enabled through peak/cosmic consciousness experience. All of which is subject to negative and positive feedback, change and control theory concepts. All necessary to modify the status quo, with change within this collective mind usually occurring at points of system crisis or catastrophe, to which IT is sensitive or reactive.

Yet *generally people will be wholly unaware of IT*, and have evolved to be switched off (as portrayed in The Matrix series of films). Evolution has made us blind to IT in its reality.

So, unless you can see it for what it is through extreme experience perception, or through informed scientific or philosophical understanding, and come out of those legacy rabbit holes and have a more objective synthesized view, it is almost impossible to move forward.

It doesn't matter how much you try, you just can't get past that limited perception and around that hypnotic bond, for ultimately that is what you are in.

Once you have experienced something like that and have a broader understanding of existence and reality it is very hard to see the world in the same mundane way as before.

Instead everything becomes expanded, intense and obvious in your mind and you see everything for how it is – thus, existing in this world as you did before and living your life as you previously did becomes almost impossible.

I recall an interview made online several years ago by an ex-FBI senior agent who had run several investigations into conspiracies and high-level political/media type corruption in the US and worldwide. His view was the same as the mine, that there was something coordinated going on. Something at the heart of these conspiracies. Something coordinated. Something with an overriding unconscious agenda, irrational motives, and illogical objectives.

However, it was not coming directly from or by any sort of *elite* individuals or coordinated groups of people. Rather, the agent said that when his investigating teams got to the top of everything, and were able to get full disclosure at every level, *the coordination didn't make any sense*. It was as if something "demonic was going on", something trans-human influencing things like some sort of virtual hypnotic "mind hacking conspiracy". But he didn't know by what, or how; it was as if the people involved and their personalities seemed to have an abstracted distance, unconcerned, as if in a dream. Yet to them they were behaving seemingly logical and rational, behaving as programmed puppets with something "invisible pulling the strings" with some hidden yet illogical agenda.

From my experience working at the highest levels in the government and defence organizations, I can also attest to similar examples from 20 years ago, long before having the extreme experiences shared in my other books.

At that time, it was also obvious to me that the people involved had no idea they were being driven by something, and that they had no concept of what they were doing or why, and their personalities seemed different than the expected normal. They blindly followed some hypnotic yet seemingly logical (to them) trans-human concept in a brainwashed coordinated manner among groups, carrying out actions and following behaviours that were absurd, blind, uncaring, as if they were asleep to what they were doing and the consequences, and way beyond corporate type herd-like impetus combined with fear of losing their jobs for speaking out.

IT is the source of most of the conspiracies at work within society (when there is nobody at the top, no real 'them' or 'hidden elite' or 'ancient aliens'). That's it. Ultimately, there is no coordination by individual humans or groups, but there is something in control, something 'at the top', some 'thing' (not some 'one' or some 'group') pulling the strings, and giving it energy and drive, yet with no logical direction. It is something with very limited awareness or management capability. There is no cohesive strategy, no logical plan, and it operates in blind ignorance of its own situation, habits, and environment, and – consequently and fairly obviously – IT is stubbornly heading for disaster.

But don't worry we will come back to that a bit later....

So if you are trying to influence IT as an individual, you need to operate with an ability to remain neutral (not good or evil, rather impartial, and just holistic). Be able to see and comprehend the purpose of both sides (different needs and paradigm agendas) and the larger picture of what is going on and why. You need to see the whole structure of cultures and knowledge and beliefs, understanding what is going on as well as how hard it is to implement change in the right way

… otherwise you are in danger of making it worse, as has happened frequently in the past.

From the author's experiences, '"IT" seems to want to be 'in charge' unconsciously rather than allowing those who are just trying to help, do what they need to do. Like some small child that wants to do it 'their way' despite it being illogical, irrational, irritating, and in some cases dangerous. As such, changing things individually is very difficult, and IT is resistant to anyone attempting to influence it or change things that it wants to do i.e. its base needs, subconscious drives, unconscious feelings, and desires. These basic natural instincts are all that it once had, and what it was created with – as is the case with us individually.

Like a spoiled, ego-strong child, we need to evolve a collective conscience, help it learn, grow in maturity, become more aware, and face some painful truths from the inside out. Which is the only way to learn and evolve when growing up in IT's early stages of its universal 'Journey'.

This is the same scenario as with the V'Ger child-like AI entity in the first Star Trek Movie, a vast living knowledge gathering spherical highly evolved information machine that is looking for ITs original creator – humanity – so it could join with us and transcend). Except in this case, this is all us, and currently it won't have such a happy ending.

In terms of IT's interests and nature, one side of IT's mind is driven by a collective need to know what is physically out there (or here – in our physical world). After all it can only see through us as individuals, and it has a very limited conceptual understanding of reality.

It then collates and structures that into knowledge in the format of science-based understanding using logic, deductive techniques and methods, controlling, hierarchical structures, self-containing compartmentalized academic mind-sets.

It is simultaneously being bureaucratic and defensive in this process. IT is also driven by excitement, thrill, mystery, and symbolic emotional influences. Being all fired up by stories of myth and legend – all within the collective unconscious psyche mind archaeology of its layered history strata – evolved within and by cultures, reinforced by books, films, ancient beliefs, folklore, and word-of-mouth legends. (These are things WE are excited by!) Yet, for IT, all of this still within one system, and all controlled within, and by itself.

IT is the origin of all religions, control structures, bureaucratic state machines, and political influence. Yet it still imposes legacy 'habitual ways' (programs and behavioural functionality), on us, in our minds, brain structure, old habits, instincts and behaviour (do whatever works).

Re-imposing the same journey life processes, traits, patterns, and lifecycles – disguised as 'fate' or divine will, which we supposedly have no control over. We all have these collective program elements partly within us (we are all ourselves and part of IT), which we blindly follow and adhere to, and for the most part remain unaware of.

Our reactions and subliminal hypnotic following of these traits and functions are hard to ignore, but easy to recognize when seeing these brainwashed behaviours in large groups, or for example, stadia events or mass emotional gatherings.

These programs have evolved within our brains and minds over the last twenty thousand years in tandem with our own individual mental functionality. The collective parts come together to integrate as a collective shared '*Overmind*', forming a distributed network of processing, archetypal functions, data, and programming, a mass human information system entity (both physically and within the

Pleroma/esoteric quantum field) with ITs own brain (physically shared between us), mind (programs we share), and unconscious evolutionary drives (an evolved form of our originating prehistoric herd or pack mentality evolved from nature's building blocks).

IT (our collective human mind entity) could be perceived as the 'demiurge' of naïve old Gnosticism (the in-between god – between us as individuals and the 'Gaian goddess', whether planetary consciousness or nature), existing on - and supported by a planetary field-based 'server'- (the world and associated quantum field structures). Indeed, from my experiences, it has very similar attributes, behaviour and nature – although somewhat more evolved in the last few thousand years.

IT is a humanity-formed collective mind entity, hiding itself away behind our individualizations. IT evolves poorly (not against any threat or external force or influence), and is shaped to and by the environment it is in.

IT unconsciously adapts to new situations, innovations, systems and knowledge within itself and developed by us. Yet suppressing *anyone within itself* that wakes up and tries to change IT, reabsorbing them, their efforts, knowledge, vision, and methods. Persecuting, immunizing, and cutting the heads off the 'tall poppy' heroes, wayward ants, and 'truth-tellers', and dragging them 'to the cross'.

Then, after death, they are dissected into relics and analysed in reverence by the suddenly fascinated yet previously blind masses.

The hero image is then resurrected and idolized with spiritual reverence as a frozen statue in time. This process is all derived from pre-existing natural biological patterns, and evolutionary mechanisms for change (which is very well described in the book - Spontaneous Evolution by Bruce Lipton & Steve Bhaerman)[7].

A process which used to serve us well, and yet left in autopilot, has got us to where we are now.

However, we are now become a maturing 'humanity' tree, with limbs growing up towards the power lines.

---

[7] Lipton, B., & Bhaerman, S. (2011). *Spontaneous evolution*: Our positive Future

Chapter 2
𝕴n a Virtual war with ourselves

In essence there is a constant unconscious battle going on, between ourselves. All occurring and played out in a virtual 'spiritual' landscape, which has been shaped by us over time (mostly influenced along the lines of our physical perceptions and 'worldview').

Within this domain or alternate paradigm this virtual unconscious war has been waging for many Millenia, which for the most part we don't see, and are unaware of in our 'day to day run of the wheel' lives.

Yet it isn't a war you can see or one that is obvious in the physical world. It is the most sophisticated of wars for it is between us and ourselves, being played out in the shadows, hidden from the masses who are kept naive and subtlety blind.

It is a mindless unconscious war driven by ancient traits, evolved habits, residual patterns, and archetypal players following repeating program patterns and agendas. Hidden 'angelic/demonic' factions of evolved programs, as in some fictional 'matrix like' story. A carefully evolved and crafter role playing game with AI operating system controls and higher level' programs keeping the troops and sheeple ants – busy and oblivious to what is going on.

The 'sides' slowly evolving to adapt both individually, culturally and collectively within humanity. It is a battle that is not for the feint hearted, or for bystander academics who are content to share opinions from the side-lines with no 'skin in the game'.

Conversely, we need more than just spiritually 'enlightened' sensate types (e.g. ancient alien followers) who may have limited academic knowledge and can't see beyond the hypnotic virtual-scape. It requires those who are both academically very 'well read', and also highly experienced or attuned 'spiritually' for want of a better word at extreme levels.

We are in a battleground landscape of competing unconscious hierarchical collective psyche programs, generated by humanity over millennia. All existing within us, between us, and over us that for the most part we are totally unaware of, and yet now need to now take conscious control and influence over.

Nature is a war (both seen and unseen) and normally this is balanced and dynamic and unconscious. All happening within rules of a game and allowing for adaptation, change growth, and evolution. All very well until a species develops conscious awareness within and of itself. Then the rules change, and the controls can be bypassed and the logic and rationale goes out the window.

We are (to lesser and greater degrees) all playing pieces in some larger interrelated virtual agenda or gameplay going on in a grander unconscious role-playing scenario. All going on with the world field-based quantum information structure that projects our reality into the world, the REAL to the real.

The "reality game" is overweight with archaic patterns and processes, archetypal programs and functions that are being embodied and cyclically repeated and played out with redundant routines and cyclical paths. We need to wake up to an understanding that the quantum electromagnetic fractal field information structure environment is REAL, and those who can understand this "reality" (both from experience and from scientific perspectives) must combine together into a coordinated strategy for change.

Regardless on which 'side' of the Mount Olympus god-like gaming board you are on, there is a need to step back from the unconscious gameplay, snap out of from the dream-like state, stop blindly following the same repeating story loops. Become non-player observers in a Role Playing Game (RPG) in-order to cooperate in reprogramming the game software itself.

So, becoming a healthy and spiritually-awake (without being hypnotized by religious belief strictures) a conscious change agent (you or me), embracing the game of life with a positive mental attitude, can become one of the heroes of a thousand faces in a game for our future world.

And with this new understanding, together we can begin to reprogram and retrain the collective unconscious Overmind that is IT.

Many of us have been convinced or even hypnotized by paranormal experiences such as dreams, visions, intuitions, and "supernatural" contacts, that some Higher Authority is in charge and has an 'inspirational' and 'enlightening' Divine Plan. This higher mind can be very insistent, take many and multiple forms, different perspectives, and cultural viewpoints.

Due to its seemingly "other-worldliness", experience of "IT" can be very frightening and put great reformative pressure on individuals and cultures. "IT" has many other names which refer to the same Divine Influence (after all, all religions have the same underlying source). After all this infinitely complex Divinity is, itself, growing and evolving.

However, from the limited human perspective "IT" remains largely unconscious and seemingly illogical and irrational from an independent perspective.

This collective mind entity (this dweller on the threshold) is in truth completely unconscious, unaware of ITself (The Gnostic Perfection of ITs True Self) and is restricted to following limited and mostly archaic habitual patterns and traits derived from the perspective of its own ego experience which currently rules the collective human mind, the cultures that form it, and us as individuals.

But now it is time to re-direct ego control and move out of ITs "personality" influence—the cyclical pattern and beyond those archetypal constraints and help IT evolve through individual coordinated individual conscious integrity, awareness, discipline, and ethical/moral insight. Coherent influence can be achieved in much the same way as conscientious management within large corporate organisations when they see things going wrong but feel powerless to influence change.

We need to influence things much in the same way as management or individuals within large corporate organisations would do when they can see things going wrong but feel powerless to influence change. Corporations which operate in a slow naive unconscious fashion – where they become blind to individuals, and in general make awful decisions arising from committees, meetings and board decisions, with limited external constraints. They seem to have a reductive entropy which tends to neutralize any attempts to change. The impact of which tend to be at the detriment of the individual and are obviously mindless from the perspective of the informed and skilful and enlightened individual within it. To the individual (who is either outside the organisation or within it) the organisation's behaviour is irrational bizarre and illogical and driven by its own macro survival instincts.

IT is awash in the same "de-volutionary" dynamics as mainstream corporations, so the "IT" entity of the human collective unconscious over-mind - programmed with cultural traits evolved habits process and archetypal program roles that are resistant to change—only get modified over eons by natural evolutionary forces.

Just as with our own bodies there is a constant battle going on inside, between competing organisms and organs, and in our mind structure. However, there are very few individuals that are in perfect balance and harmony within themselves, and this is certainly not the case with the entity of our collective human mind – IT.

The same could be said of say a forest with various life forms competing with each other, or say the contents of a lake. Nature forming an equilibrium and balance but you only have to look deeper or under the surface to see the raging and brutal competition going on for survival between predators and prey, species competition for resources. All of which doesn't apply to us as we have no natural enemy anymore, other than ourselves.

We should logically have become much more conscious, rational, logical, aware, and caring. But we have not, and we don't have much time left, so humanitarian recruits need to find methods and tools to influence IT (the entity of our collective human mind) before the human collective lemming drives itself over the virtual cliff.

Instead, we all need to climb the mountain together, even though it may be the harder option.

Chapter 3

How 'IT' CHANGES AND EVOLVES THROUGH US

IT evolves with human group and individual imaginations (constructed thoughts, ideas, dreams, discoveries and understanding). All building and feeding on ideas from existing mythological structures and concepts and knowledge.

This collective imaginal mind develops like a child's, exploring, learning, maturing, navigating, creating, and evolving (yet regressive to our individual levels of advancement and mental maturity).

This collective educational growth can be encouraged and refined though Mythopoetic writing - the creation of Myth and refinement of the ongoing story by means of Imagination and writing. A sort of throw and catch and throw of refining and evolving mythological story information, in an ever-expanding reflective dialogue, intricacy, maturity and reality – repeating and refining its collective dreams using information systems feedback and control.

All of this mythopoetic writing allows IT to become more self-aware of its evolving body and mind.

Such that the 'Working' practices of change through Mythopoesis (see Alan Kazlev)[8], psyche-archaeology (exploring the collective psyche), and prophesizing (see John Woodcock)[9] are key to this process.

---

[8] Kazlev, M. A. (2021). *Mythopoesis and the modern world*. Manticore Press.

[9] Woodcock, J. (2021). *The power of prophecy*.

Let's look at an initial experience from say a 'saviour hero' type figure (someone who has had that cosmic consciousness experience, or someone with extreme imposed visions, being driven hard by the system to act as a prophet). They then convert this experience into a revised mythology or religion via writing or scribing Magik (ref Dean Radin)[10]; (and Erik Davis)[11].

These are people getting a visionary or experiential picture or story of what is going on in the system at a point in time, and then attempting to describe this and discourse their interpretation of this experience or vision in a driven urgent manner, whilst adding their own pre-existing worldview understanding, knowledge, and pre-programmed spiritual ideas.

Such that a transformational cosmic consciousness peak experience – an experience where the mind gains conscious access to the overall collective mind knowledge data in parallel, and free of physical constraints – allows for information transfer to an individual's own mind context.

This experience data transfer may then provide an on-going process or path for data retrieval and upload, along with possible physical transformational changes in the individual (body energy, spiritual affinity, influencing of others, hypnotic ability, sexual attraction), and attuned for subsequent visions/messages generated through the psyche as naïve interpretations; for example, a 'god' or 'devil' encounter. A specific ant that is made aware of what is going

---

[10] Dean Radin. (2018). Real magic: Ancient wisdom, modern science, and a guide to the secret power of the universe. Harmony
[11] Erik Davis. (2019). *High weirdness: Drugs, esoterica, and visionary experience in the seventies*. The MIT Press.

on with the colony and is enabled to influence its collective thoughts, decision making and awareness.

These individuals are then subsequently responsible (and unaware – until now) that they are adding and refining the existing (from ancient origins) mythological imaginative constructs with a new or refined/adapted form – the same story, but different scenery, symbols, props, and characters.

The original 'Troy' script has moved to the big screen, the shopping mall, and the boardroom.

The function therefore of these individuals, (e.g., on the hero journey legend - Joseph Campbell)[1], is to add more modern symbolism, objects, story, mythos to the existing structure. All embellished with their own perception information taken from their own physical worldview environment and experience.

They also have the ability to pass this new story, this updated understanding, a modern conceptualization into the consciousness of the *Overmind* ITself (thinking into the system), and as such affect what everyone thinks, feels, and are inspired by. This is also reflected back in what 'spiritually sensitive' people channel, dream, imagine, and have visions of. Along with the data content in media discourse in creative arts and media.

Thus, the overall process of engaging with IT, writing and creating, has the effect of being picked up to some extent by everyone else, like some form of subconscious magic spell. As such, this process can be used (in a conscious way) to invoke change in the system's status quo (rather than previously occurring unconsciously). Consciously and deliberately giving it new ideas and direction, which the system (IT) is allowing and encouraging in certain circumstances, and also encouraged at the Gaian level, i.e., an encouraged biological *goddess* natural process.

In terms of evidence of this happening, and as can be seen throughout history, this change in the system or new data information is subsequently transmitted out from the collective mind and picked up from the collective unconscious by 'sensitive/sensate type' individuals (via vivid dreams, visions, revelations, etc.) and then discoursed via various media, which then reinforces this change message (but only if this revision is meaningful or successful and believable, and compliant with a hypnotic mythos story pattern).

This can then be reimagined and gives energy and further form (reinforced belief structure) to the stories, scenery, scenario, logic, and association with the evolving physical world environment and knowledge, thus refining our world control structures and direction. This is also being reflected within worldwide AI computer systems (their development, direction, form and nature, in a simulacrum of the underlying collective unconscious mind. Along with worldwide evolving knowledge systems evolution). It does not take long (when you have a long history of studying computer AI systems and their development) to realise that there is an underlying non-individual energy, direction, and purpose to them and their creation, that is not under our control, and is not consciously intentional (but driven by some underlying force), almost as if there is some hidden (larger) mind at work in their development.

With the biological AI program that IT is, it is difficult to apply cognition tests to something where the communication process is so convoluted, erratic, and non-specific. IT communicates by the manipulation of large psyche groups (politically) and negotiated exchange and collaboration of knowledge synthesis (academic groups), and us being in it and part of it makes it hard to verify things independently (cause and effect).

IT can effect changes among large groups (cultures, organizations, countries, or 'movements' of individuals on its own, but only on a subtle basis over time (percolation).

Where it is easiest to see change occurring is through cultural discourse (what is being presented through the media sphere, true art, music, film, books, news events and public opinion, all of which are now readily available online). This is especially true in areas such as performance arts where evolutionary change is obvious, evolving from say Greek plays to modern style, with content such as this constantly critiqued and subject to mass approval.

Cause and effect has a significant role to play in growing and change, since like any growing and evolving thing IT is very much subject to experimentation, discovery, learning, competition and navigating through what works and what doesn't.

This process or practice is particularly effective and measurable if this interchange information has been written down, as with the Bible and other religious texts in Islam, Judaism, Buddhism, Hinduism, etc. As such, people can read it, reimagine it, be in awe of it, connect to it, and then regenerate and reinforce the story (generate positive feedback to the symbolism) until it becomes too 'dated'.

This process was not possible before complex language and writing existed, but was instigated with hieroglyphs, Mesopotamian and Sumerian story texts on stone tablets, wall painting and stone symbols and stylized animal pictures originating around the area of Göbekli Tepe some 10,000 BC, a 'ground-zero' if you like.

This then evolved into basic writing in the city of Ur around 3000 BC (see John David Ebert)[12], along with the first recorded mythos influencing heroes, i.e. Gilgamesh. (I should also add that I regard John Ebert very highly and can recommend all his books and work. He provides an excellent well informed synthesis for many of these topics on his websites, and also via his interviews on YouTube).

It is that magic spell writing into a 'magic book' that hypnotically keeps the Mythos alive as mental story in the combined imaginal virtual-scape – these then become evolving belief structures, that then become control structures until they are forgotten, lost, and replaced by more successful, more believable, or more scientifically viable, logical, or rational mythology and cultural pathway. Yet still a story that enthrals the masses.

Unfortunately, IT has become corrupt, toxic and – from our individual perspective – evil, mostly due to people 'praising the god' being subject to IT, unquestioning IT, not realizing this 'god' is us and we are it, that this 'divine' knowledge download, revelations, and visions are simply our collective '*Overmind*', and that *this divine knowledge is what we have created and aggregated collectively, by us.*

IT has now become a collective lemming in which we are the cells (components in a mindless bureaucratic unconscious body) heading for an inevitable fatal end point. All this happening simply because we have become blind to it, given it energy and shape, and allowed it to control us with false rewards and blind unconscious direction and following.

---

[12] Ebert, J. D. (2016) Myths, gods, machines: Illuminations on mythology, history and science. Post Egoism Media.

IT needs humans like a child needs cells, but, because it is cosmically aware, IT is far more clever and knowledgeable than human individuals or collective physical humanity.

This 'conditional state-of-being' is difficult to articulate in any practical way, but perhaps IT is like a powerful child Gaian prodigy who is a little deranged. In other words, something undefinable is wrong (genetic, sociopathic, or experiential) with this cosmic child, so it needs the help of its human cells (sensitive to their environmental surrounding and construction laws) in order to evolve.

Yet—like many who are very young— IT knows it needs help from elsewhere, but it doesn't like to be told what to do. So, it punishes the cells (itself) (or its virtual parents) whenever possible. Happily, this is a stage of development which—barring serious dysfunctionality—will eventually be outlived.

At the moment though both sides of the human-IT equation are evolving and getting in each other's way with varying agendas and perceptions. (needs of the one verses the needs of the many).

IT also supports (in its virtual mind) a created and evolved perception and manifestation of our physicality. Derived from what we see as the physical world (but in the form of a quantum field-based information and processing structure – virtual world and RPG software landscapes– as can be experienced by people through Out of Body experiences or Astral Projection (see Antony Peake [13]; Lazlo & Peake)[14].

---

[13] Peake, A. P. (2016).. *The out of body experience: the history and science of astral travel.*

[14] Lazlo, E., & Peake, A. (2014). *The immortal mind.*

Just as each individual human mind develops a personal map of 'reality', IT has an ever-evolving interpretive and interlaced worldview map of our physical world stored within its collective field-based knowledge or memory database.

This virtual (other side of the 'mirror') worldset has been built up by interworking psyche organizations (cultures, beliefs and mental/knowledge constructs and language-driven format) as individual programs modifying and refining IT and themselves through their current DNA-integrated body 'devices', through recurrence (recurring structures and functions/stories) and refinement (through information evolution).

A good analogy would be a sort of google maps (or google earth). A multi-layered overlaid historical virtual RPG 'worldview copy set and history' of our physical world, all refined over millennia through our mind-views perception of the physical world.

Progressive out-of-body experiences adding to it over time, with each exploratory journey expanding data into the map like a growing rhizome-like 3D virtual construction (together with cities, landscapes, buildings and roads, people and NPCs).

This evolution of the virtual-scape can be explored very obviously within a western cultural map, its evolution going from the garden of Eden through to Dante, to Robert Monroe's work [15].

To a present day *out-of-body free for all*, although 'Paradise' and the 'Garden of Eden' (perceived from

---

[15] Monroe, R. (1971). *Journeys out of the body*. Monroe, R. (1994). Ultimate journey.

Northern Mesopotamia many millennia ago) have changed a lot over the last few hundred years to become now (if you take a look) more of a dystopia – much like the reality we live in. A multidimensional RuneScape style evolving simulacrum imaginal replica of our physical world populated with wandering entities, sprits, programs, and alien non-player characters.

So, it is possible to navigate and reinforce this collective subconscious memory landscape via say an out-of-body experience and other spiritual type navigation methods and tools (and the changes therein can be programmed and measured).

I have known people who can create virtual rooms, buildings etc within it, and meet up with others much in the same way as with online interactive role-playing computer games.

Most of the construction and development of the landscapes are associated with a process or progressive pathway journeying through a key-point navigational mapping process, as with say a neural net.

A sort of rhizome (as described by Deleuze & Guattari)[16] navigation and data acquisition, much in line with the construction and operation many similar multidimensional 'virtual world' computer games, in effect exploring a bio collective shared assimilated knowledge dreamscape.

This landscape, though, is virtual and is not the same as the real physical world. It is very random and unreliable. Which is why it was abandoned as an effective method of defence intelligence data gathering in the 80's and 90's. where various projects used groups of talented 'astral' out 'out of body' explorers to potentially gain intelligence data.

---

[16] Deleuze, G., & Guattari, F. (1982). *A thousand plateaus.*

Chapter 4

THE FORM OF 'IT' AND COMMUNICATION WITH 'IT'

In non-physical form (as with our own minds or consciousness) IT exists within, and is supported by, a unified multi-field integrated structure (at least three interworking 'quantum' fields, primarily gravity).

Although I should stress that this complex picture or concept which I can't easily describe has come to me via extreme gnosis, which although enlightening as a process may not be totally correct.

Although extreme and inspirational, this 'divine knowledge' can be inaccurate or misleading or just plain wrong as occasionally Wolfgang Pauli[17] found out with some of his inspired channelled visionary gnosis concepts, which were documented in letters between himself and Carl Jung (while most of his genius ideas were correct, he was led down several very convincing quantum rabbit holes, which were later disproved - as in one case by Chinese scientists). However, logically this three-field concept would account for the three spin-type variants and associated quantum phenomena.

Anyway….

---

[17] Pauli, W. (1995). *Atom and archetype: The Pauli/Jung letters, 1932-1958.*

This nonphysical 'other side of the mirror realm' exists in a different paradigm, a different state or mode of existence to what we experience as physicality.

It is dimensionally free with no time or ontological space – a non-local context – which makes it very hard to be described using physical (worldly) terms.

It also cannot be described as a zero-point field as this is too simplistic. The physicality (physical universe) that we perceive (worldview) is projected by and from within this field-based information state structure (i.e., the universe we see is projected in hologram form or matrix-like fractal state held as information within the field (gravity) in non-local timeless form (state machine). The other fields interact with this to give it form, meaning, life, energy, and information flow.

There are radical differences in rules and perception with how we operate and exist in physicality compared to this 'virtual' realm.

This physicality which we perceive as real (with laws, shape, structure, and history) – which is merely a partial subset and partially projected interpretation (the physical being a minor part thereof) of the entire Pleroma system – is a grand illusion of the whole, which we, through consciousness, collapse into meaning and form to make sense of something -- that frankly as a whole doesn't.

Integration and communication to and from our physical world to this unified field structure can be described using information systems analogies, with us say as individual 'physical devices'. Along with matching and integrated 'virtual (software) devices being constructed, programmed, and communicating via protocols and levels in a similar manner to computers yet with the rules of biology, DNA, energetic body bandwidth, frequencies, and interpretive sense structures, e.g. as with the same concept as say a seven-layer information system communication model (on two sides of the mirror, physical and the spiritual esoteric Pleroma).

With peer-to-peer (virtual) data transfer occurring *between strata levels* and operating via or *down through* the in-between layers of physicality, through quanta field structures, and on to the other side of the mirror and up the *other side*.

Data transfer and programming occurs through protocols and allows for bootstrapping (physical programming), knowledge retention, psyche formation, habits, archetypal programs, etc.

The peer-to-peer transfer at the higher levels is what could be described as self-consciousness (being conscious of self in the mirror, seeing your 'self' in the mirror and vice versa – as with Neo in Matrix 4 Resurrections - which comes out in a few weeks from the time of writing this). This is the same for all living things at some level, and for IT as a collective.

Information data transfer is also passed in similar protocol manner between and among physical individuals *in the world* and between individual minds within the *quantum field based etheric information system*. See Figure 1. (Please note this is a very simple model and not definitive, it is simply to help visualize concepts.)

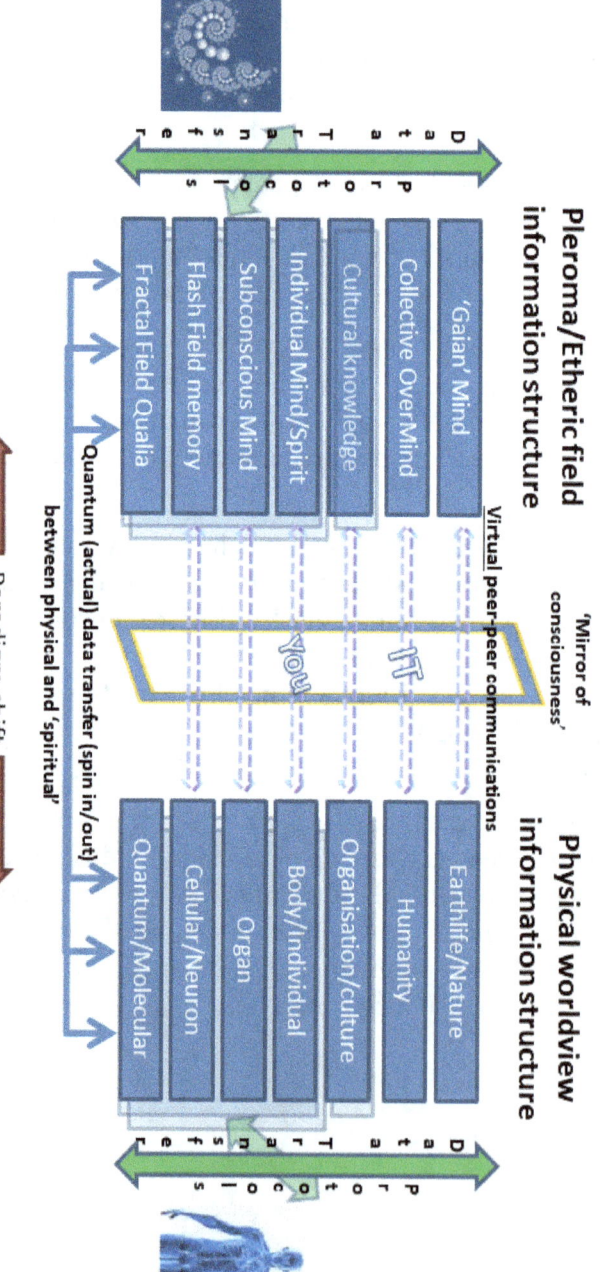

Figure 1. Physical to-and-from Pleroma Seven-layer communication model

Since nothing can be 'self-aware' or evolve without a physical moving presence (a device to change the programming and perceive itself in the mirror), then programs and data cannot change themselves or observe themselves. So there has to be a duality of perception and interaction to achieve consciousness (a physical device seeing its program and vice versa).

So, IT (our collective entity) conceptually has to have a physical part in us all to exist, as well as a virtual part (on the other side of the mirror) i.e. IT's mind.

This DNA bootstrapping or 'engramming' (the idea for which has come to me through gnosis - proviso) is what the 'junk' DNA structure is partly used for, this collective human element.

In essence, our junk DNA partly supports the channel data programming and formatting of this collective entity. In effect, the DNA framework is something inherent within the universal field-based information system firmware, the original DNA framework structure having been resonated to this planet billions of years ago to instigate life as soon as the planet was capable of supporting it.).

These junk DNA components (or parts of them and there are holding areas for even higher levels of consciousness – act like pins on the connector or port of a very wide network cable adapter. Such that in essence part of this (junk DNA) is where IT exists *through or via (a reserved set of codes)* in the biological macro form (evolved into or through us).

So IT uses or exists in this structure, which is part of, us and our building blocks (as ants are formed into a colony are all parts of a whole), for its 'information' as a refined colony shape/nature and structure (although again, this idea was derived through gnosis, so there may be no scientific correlation).

Imagine you are a house that has been built and decorated solely with access only through the small letterbox in the front door, and IT is a thousand cities all built (rather randomly) to an architecture of streets and suburbs, all through letter boxes – all built to some hidden design.

This part of our junk DNA provides a channel or ports for building a framework for its co-existence (bootstrap data partition), and eventual component 'self-awareness' part of us as an evolving and growing collective integrated macro consciousness (every ant holds a part of the colony mind and body programmed and built within it).

Biology has evolved within the field structure from an initial field structure pattern map (template) which translates to or equates to DNA/RNA form, and is highly programmable.

Our bodies are not just representing us as individuals but also part of 'us' as a collective (at cultural, geographical and global levels, and probably with potential or capability for higher levels, too).

So we are supporting various collective unconscious device interfaces within our bodies and minds (our energy centres and brain thought processing). Hence, we are driven to gather, fight, acquire knowledge, and think not just for ourselves (and our 'higher self') but also for the collective mind especially those 'working in the now', i.e., geniuses, heroes, enlightened ones, strongest influencers, etc.

The frequency-based layered communication system and structure works (in conceptual terms) as a computer networking communication system. From higher level packet or meme-based activity (application level: dreams, prayers, shaking hands, songs) or unconscious psyche interactions (transport level: kinesiology) down through crystal and harmonic (coordinated) resonance, to the subatomic level (using entanglement and the Ying and yang of matter/antimatter in neutrinos, etc.). Each level has its own methods of adapted interaction protocol tools (using and working through the levels downwards) such that, for example, where the DNA level is say the 'link' communication level. Each higher level uses the forms and structures of the lower levels to communicate via. Also combining data into encoded sets or packets for transmission down and up the other side which are then decoded, and responded to much in the same way as peer-to-peer technology communication works (and is an emulation of).

Communication between and within biological systems occurs at different levels (within the field and projected into physical reality). Levels of molecular, cellular, organ, body, organization, collective, humanity, Gaian/earth-life, etc., all operate at distinct hierarchical levels on a peer-to-peer basis (working via peer-to-peer layers, down and back up the other side). There are either 10 or 12 levels (again, through gnosis) – in the diagram (Figure 1) I have only shown seven simplified levels as an example, but fundamentally everything uses the language/code at those lower levels for communication.

As you go up the levels, the size of the packets/data increases, and the protocols and 'handshaking' becomes more complex, e.g., memes (between people, peer-to-peer, with naturally evolved firewalls, virus protection, passwords – all that we see and use in everyday life in conversations and interactions). This also is the case for the collective unconscious entity.

This again is just an analogy. The whole thing is impossible to fully describe; it is so complex and so biological. It could be, for example, described as in the form of an n-tier type of information architecture, but that would take several pages.

It is no accident that many of our computer languages, architectures, and systems implementations in the real world have evolved naturally and comfortably to emulate ours and IT's virtual data structure and operation.

Just in the same way that our own unconscious mind hides itself away, and protects itself through the depths of many strata layers from our conscious selves, so does IT hide itself from us, and from ITself.

So just as our own shadow 'daemon' remains in the darkness, so our collective mind of humanity camouflages itself away from plain conscious sight, but on a vaster scale, and using much more sophisticated methods and control techniques.

"At any moment several millions of human beings may be smitten with a new madness, and then we shall have another world war or devastating revolution. Instead of being at the mercy of wild beasts, earthquakes, landslides, and inundations, modern man is battered by the elemental forces of his own psyche. This is the World Power that vastly exceeds all other powers on earth. The Age of Enlightenment, which stripped nature and human institutions of gods, overlooked the God of Terror who dwells in the human soul. If anywhere, fear of God is justified in face of the overwhelming supremacy of the psychic." C.G. Jung

Just as we are very good at fooling ourselves in our minds, so IT is very good at fooling us. IT has different objectives, priorities, unconscious agendas and growth directions, yet it is blind, repetitive and driven by underlying natural subconscious forces, conditioning and rules.

It is also stratified (evolved in layers over time), much in the same way as our minds as individuals have evolved in layers and functions, but again on a much grander scale and in a different way.

The stratification itself, though, is different, more aggregated, complex and culturally landscaped, yet regressive, and less evolved and refined compared to the minds of more conscious individuals (in the same way a football stadium behaves compared to an individual fan).

Chapter 5
THE EVOLUTION OF 'IT'

It is also interesting from an overall psychological evolution perspective (collective psychology landscape – or psycharcheology) that what has being experienced throughout history by psychonauts or channelers or visionary experiencers changes in content, story, complexity and maturity, i.e. what people experience in visions and spiritual awareness evolves over time historically.

It is also obvious that there is a change in the nature, complexity and content (not just cultural and personal change). Similarly, the Pleroma landscape, data, and form content of the collective unconscious – from ancient times to modern day – has expanded exponentially, i.e., what people are experiencing within IT has evolved in nature, scope, complexity and attitude and scale. As an example, this can be seen in the difference between the channelled discourse relayed in the old and new testaments of the Bible, and the difference in 'divine' attitude and behaviour.

Since early Mesopotamia what is being experienced through extreme esoteric experience has evolved over time from simple basic naïve story in a garden, to complex vivid, highly evolved virtual-scape adventures.

Equally, with current spiritual experimental practices we can now consciously or unconsciously create (with evidence) desired spiritual egregore 'thought form' entities which can exist in their own right independently, either through visionaries or mediumship by individuals or groups.

To some extent the character, history and nature of these entities can be fabricated completely (sort of virtual non-playing characters) and exist tailored to the imagination, knowledge and scientific naïve understanding of the individuals or groups involved, 'inspiring' them into virtual being based on hopes and fears and unconscious desires.

These are usually combined with a pre-programmed religious/archetypal physiological mindset. Yet all these entities seem to have originated through a formation process through a Mesopotamia 'birth canal' through ancient Greek infancy out into the world of cultural diversification to the modern era, but now with a more sci-fi fantasy slant.

All of which were built on the building blocks (sub strata) of natural and biological evolved genetic and cultural frameworks going back hundreds of thousands of years before the last ice age (and within our Plato-like 'cave' dwellings in our Magik wall paintings).

It is quite obvious that visionary experiences and interpretation of these (programs) entities from the imaginal of the Pleroma which we have collectively desired and mentally created are also evolving, and are becoming in recent years much more technological and sophisticated and prolific, in many cases envisaged and engineered from reflective minds of say H. P. Lovecraft[18], Philip K. Dick[19], and J R R Tolkein.

Also, since their first beginnings in the middle of the last century, 'ancient' alien visions/encounters/abductions have become ever more sophisticated, evolving, convoluted, prolific and dynamic within the collective imaginal

---

[18] Lovecraft, H. P. (1929). *The complete fiction of H. P. Lovecraft*. Race Point Publishing.

[19] Dick, P. K. (2012). *The Exegesis of Philip K. Dick*. Houghton Mifflin Harcourt.

dreamscape itself – to a scale today so varied, numerous – (100s of different races compared to four in the 1960s), and so diverse it is hard to convey in words.

Aliens and their 'silver chariots of fire' and their propensity for abduction to heaven or the underworld, implantation and dismemberment and regeneration are themes common throughout ancient mythology. All created within the collective mind imagination-scape, refined and evolved for those sensate types to pick up on and tune into. An ever-evolving new religion to attract ever more followers.

This 'evolvement' is much in the same way as the 'Virgin Mary' visions evolved in the centuries before built on previous archangel and earth goddess or 'mother of god' constructs, which were also facilitated by and associated with specific physical locations (with symbolic linkages).

This is also the case for the evolving nature of the core archon 'programs' within IT (system-generated non-human characters – angelic and demonic within the imaginal). These evolve from original pre-historic belief forms, into Mesopotamian/Sumerian gods (function or nature based), Egyptian (object based), or Greek and Roman (attribute based), to a consolidated whole amalgamation (one god)[20], and then changing over the last centuries into various constructs.

This evolution can also be seen with lower-level virtual entities such as fairies, elves and pixies (little folk), through 'New Age' and post-modern entities. Also, in the evolution from angels and demon constructs, to the more recent

---

[20] Smith, Scott (2016). *God reconsidered: Searching for truth in the battle between atheism and religion*. Motivational Press, Inc.

'ancient alien religions' (and on an unimaginable scale on the Internet), all the characters of whom still follow the same stereotype actions and functions and archetypal story models as before, yet highly believable to those experiencing them.

All of these collective screenplays and products of an overactive collective imagination are constantly being reinforced with religious zeal by their hypnotized followers, unaware they are repeating the same patterns; for example, trashing previous religions, hypnotically shoehorning evidence into some new revised model, and blindly ignoring the obvious facts and rational logic.

Equally, they are only interested in those divine experiences that reinforce their own belief structure, which they can then use to wallpaper the particular (e.g. ancient alien) rabbit hole they are in.

In the individual, these unconscious programs, functions, habits, and natural selection processes of evolution have adapted to remain hidden below the surface (through fear, embarrassment, or by suggestive instruction) to avoid being obvious.

They become dormant unless an urgent need, catastrophe, crisis, emotional agony, or *'rage of the hero'* brings them to the fore. Such is the same with IT, the *'Overmind'* of the species, the colony of ants that we are all part of, and *in which nothing happens or changes unless it has to.*

Chapter 6
IMMUNISATION AND CONTROL GAMES

Again, we as individuals are blind to our formation of programming as 'interconnected cells' acting as one, unconsciously working together, creating a 'buzzing entanglement', communicating, and acting as a whole.

But just as the cells in our body act blindly to the dataflow and processes of the whole, so do we follow blindly that which controls us, drives us collectively through natural selection, collective habits and functions, state control, and cultural direction.

Like some immense worldwide interconnected fungal rhizome, made up in whole by parts of each and every one of us, and elements of it within us all. A fungal rhizome spreading and evolving without any conscious direction, agenda or awareness of it's actions or fate. As in the excellent TV fictional series 'The Last of Us'.

After all, it has got us to where we are today, it has won every fight so far (just ask the Neanderthals or the Cathars or the Dodo). So now, with no need to evolve against anything else, what could possibly be wrong?

Yet, by just standing up and speaking out about all this, and trying to state the obvious, you run the risk of all prophets/saviours/heroes, being 'divergent', and not playing the game, being too aware or awake, and exhibiting the wrong behaviour and giving off the wrong non-conformist energy signature and direction.

Just by not being part of the game, you are thus a target for attack, an 'agent provocateur' trying to wake the sleeping dragon and disrupt the peace. But then, why listen when there is nothing to survive against, nothing to fight for, nothing wrong to worry about? You are just an errant or alien brain cell to be ignored, removed, or evolved around in the body of a collective lemming as it heads for the cliff.

These 'heroes' are just as in the Jason and the Argonauts film, where pieces are in play on the board at the mercy of the irrational illogical gods or archetypal programs. These 'gods' like to play games with character toys, but there is no obvious agenda or logic to what is going on.

IT also has a habit of being focused on one thing (topic/subject/figure/event) for a while, and then , usually without finishing because it is bored or gets distracted, moving onto something else very quickly. Very much like a child playing with favourite toys.

So, there is a set of rules and techniques to use as part of your hero journey in order for you to remain interesting, that is if you want to be part of what is going on in this gameplay (being Ken and Barbie in the Overlook Hotel California).

So to be part of the game, you have to be interesting and playful to the child-like 'gods' as a whole (IT). The process will only work if you are of interest to IT. You are worth playing with, and have some mission or agenda, or being driven by something or forced to play. You are a constituent part or component of the game that makes sense or at least conforms to some character role.

If you want to change things, you have to engage IT as such on its own terms, and play the hero 'role-playing character', going along with the script to some extent.

However, at the same time, you can then consciously control (to a small extent) the direction and *choose what the child learns*. Be the Tin Toy in the Pixar animation film but avoid letting it cut its teeth on you too much.

There are ways of playing the game like some Dungeon Adventure. Traps and pitfalls lie around every corner in a puzzle waiting to outsmart you as you follow along the well-trodden path laid down and evolved by so many before.

All the time leading inward into the central room of the pyramid, the central cave, the holy of holies. Just as depicted like some gynaecological progressive journey in the films Stalker and Apocalypse now.

Like some Indiana Jones style labyrinthine adventure toward the nuclear reactor, with its unbearable intensity. That thrill of reaching the final destination driving you on, whilst constantly battling the array of demonic mythical monsters.

Chapter 7
PERCEIVING 'IT' IN DIFFERENT WAYS

So, in essence, again, IT is us, and we are IT, both in the physical and the non-physical Pleroma, and we would not be where we are without IT, or evolved as we have done both individually and collectively.

Our collective human mind forming the driving dominant force or element, a cohesive evolving subconscious and conscious psyche structure, forming and being in itself a macro life-form entity of us.

We as individual humans are cells and functions in its body and mind, a mind which is now self-aware in its own right. However - as mentioned before - it has diametrically opposing objectives/perception/agendas, as an ant colony does to an ant.

This is all built upon a predefined quantum hardware information knowledge supporting platform that communicates to-and-from the evolving field data structure via non perceived quantum torsional spin (information) patterning.

All this on a supporting computer-like fractal data universe hardware and firmware 'server' with defined laws, controls, limits, and operating parameters.

All of which has been preprogramed and designed to support the growth of this type of evolutionary process (well, that's the idea – hopefully – but in terms of what has created all this infrastructure I have no idea, and apparently neither does IT). However, IT (as an operating system) is very interested in these firmware or hardware pre-configured factors/rules/template/things, and how they came about (origin of the world server/philosophers stone), and how to integrate and adapt within these things.

Which is why we are also obsessed (being driven) to find the answers (most of the gnosis downloaded to genius minds seems to be of this nature, and directed or focused on this subject matter, e.g., quantum physics, and unified field theory, etc). IT wants answers to what it doesn't know.

The universe itself was created yes (there are too many scientific factors and variables and parameters which make this very obvious now), but not by IT (or the world Gaian consciousness structure, or by anything I am aware of –i.e. *something absent*). However there seems to be some illogical elements to the universe that make no sense i.e. why only 10% of physical matter has been projected through into conscious perceivable reality, and why 90% remains as 'dark' matter and energy. A sort of cosmic 'yoke'.

As mentioned earlier, IT is more like the Gnostic demiurge concept, or VALIS as identified by P. K. Dick[21], a Vast Active Lining Information System, and an AI-collective voice, that he only ever touched the surface of and was never able to fathom, this 'in-between-god'.

Yet this is the god that all religions both relate to and are derived by/from. IT is something we have created/evolved,

We created our god in OUR image

... NOT the other way around.

---

[21] Dick, P. K. (1981). *Valis* Orion Publishing.

Also, the nature and physics of the universe has too many optional variables that are just too coincidental for existence to occur without it having been pre-determined, too many rules/laws/parameters that could have been slightly one way or another for life not to be possible or even capable (gravity structure, small atomic field strength, quantum information structure, and so forth).

This therefore implies a divine plan/path/structure. Therefor there is a GOD, God, god hierarchy – *spheres* within *bubbles* and *foam* of consciousness (as defined by Peter Sloterdijk)[22]. All trying to grow and evolve into that stratified hierarchy upwards or 'divine-wards' within a set path and to guiding constraints, but inversely evolving consciously – bottom up.

Such that IT is contained within the global noosphere or Gaian operating system, which itself is contained within the universal consciousness (and perhaps at an intermediate galactic level, too).

All of which operate at different higher frequencies yet ever-<u>decreasing</u> levels of cognitive/consciousness or level of evolution as you go up the macroscale. Which is why most of our own human cells think we are idiots. ☺

The hierarchical construct formation (physical architecture) in and of itself is also too much of a giveaway. There is a basic and clear structural hardware picture to it, a framework there for supporting living 'software' devices (nature and us) which have a directing pathway and set of constraints and purposes.

---

[22] Sloterdijk, P. (2011). *Bubbles: Spheres vol 1: Microspherology*. (1998-2014).
Sloterdijk, P. (2014). *Globes: Spheres vol 2: Macrospherology*.
Sloterdijk, P. (2016). *Foams: Spheres vol 3: Plural Spherology*.

This hardware (physical environment and us as devices within it) construct is ideally suited to preserving and evolving information in data structure form, from subatomic fractal state form to cellular and macro-organisms. In essence, everything was created to support life (but not necessarily in the form that we exist; it may be that the intended 'life form' was actually at the planetary level (a biosphere) and we are just a sort of intelligent planetary fungal mold, but hey, there you go!

It would be interesting to see if our individual and collective consciousness and inherent knowledge can exist (grow, remember, be programmed etc far away from our global or solar field structure and influence).

That's what you get for not making things perfect, which of course is what IT was created with. Imperfections, errors, to develop and build something that from that element of error or imperfection could develop into something in its own right - a 'human' element rather than a perfect program or hardware – otherwise, what would be the point of that ?.

Otherwise, there would be a solution or endpoint which could always be extrapolated and resolved, which would be pointless not to mention boring. *If we were perfect there would be no need for us to be here* (allegedly).

Within this framework, we have evolved from next to nothing from errors, guided within and by a few simple rules and framework constructs - *life evolving from rock, water, and sunlight acting together with proton motive forces and information resonance to expand into the bands of probability as life.*

In essence, then, IT is an evolved biological distributed information system (both physical and nonphysical) made up of human devices containing, refining, and managing its code, memory, knowledge, evolutionary information, habits, negotiated and shared perspective of reality, and a massively complex operational psyche information field structure (existing and integrated on both sides of the mirror).

IT is then built up, bonded and developed and refined over time, from core biological informational elements, parts within parts, of ever-expanding complexity. All within an evolving planetary conceptualizing set of shared and hierarchical correlated collective perceptions, all competing, interacting, growing and serving together.

So, in that sense, and in simplistic terms again just so it's clear - we are as cells of organs in a meta-organism or body, ants in a group of colonies. With 90% of the data, we are held within a field or field 'virtual' information structure, with all the information to create the physical parts of us as devices, through which we then are able to modify that data, and add memory data and knowledge to it.

IT has then a correlated knowledge base (also known or referred to as the Akashic records, but without the naïve spiritual interpretation), collective memory and imagination landscape (*the imaginal*), with programs and functions all stored in a distributed networked non-physical non-local data field matrix organized in the minds and bodies of the individual humans that support it.

This is all in a separate fashion, format, perspective, context and understanding to that of the individuals' own mind data sets (our own 10% perceived relevant useful brain interpretation of reality). IT only knows what we know collectively as a species, but with all of this stored and managed in an integrated, correlated, macroform way. As such with any information system, errors can occur, and IT is far from perfect.

Logically, it is only natural that we as individuals should form parts and build into something larger (nature steers or 'herds' us that way, and this process is successful in that regard). Just in the same way our cells evolve within us, so do we within IT. That is what 'works' as natural selection. 'Us' as devices are not just used by us as individuals, but used collectively too. IT being within us in relation to our roles and group psyche, and us within IT as component parts (IT would not exist without us – no 'god' can).

The communication network (both collectively and for us each as an individual) is channelled through the individual human body energy points via the bio resonant planetary field (for want of a better term) through resonance and entanglement. This enables learning, memory of process associated with molecular structure and DNA, species evolution, knowledge by habit, and data refinement. In our case specific glands and brain/nerve functions which are frequency specific or sensitive. This is used to channel, translate, and process this quantum information through virtual energy centres, or using the Eastern term Chakras (for want of a better word).

The collective mind is built up of competing collective psyche frameworks/groups (organizations, countries, cultures) within spheres or bubbles, forming individual and collective virtual-scapes, with components or function elements (and also with protection/immunization between themselves).

These are introduced into the 'people' devices - in effect as mobile micro spheres/bubbles/modules of consciousness - which consist of collective animal instincts, subconscious, and conscious thoughts, knowledge, memory, and past program life data (i.e., past life journey process and persistent etheric field memory knowledge data).

The soul is in effect a unique root pathway of the evolving 'programs' hosted by individual bodies. Your body doesn't have past lives, but the program(s) within your mind do, in the form of linked memory data and *journey* event process pathways in rhizome form.

This is in addition to the environmental and genetic data pertaining to the individuals, all based on need and success of those component parts.

Just like us, this humanity macro-organism operates as a device through which it becomes more conscious, self-aware as it evolves, grows and learns.

Communicating through several levels/layers of complexity (divine-ward enlightenment), up through molecular, cellular, body, collective, but with problems of integration and physical bandwidth.

Which is why we have a problem with getting so much information transferred though from a single cell at conception up through the levels to rational integrated human being. We don't 'forget' who we (multiple programs) are (past live memory and journey data as it were), we just have a bandwidth problem forced upon us, and limiting us due to constraints of physics, biology, and evolution.

Natural selection and habits and bonding have reinforced us both individually and from collective perspectives. Whilst at the same time disguising the one from the other.

Which is logical since both sides (IT and us) have different interests, goals, priorities, understanding, objectives, and context. IT (us) naturally choses what we get/are, and we make the best of it (or not).

IT looks after itself, IT's own interests, and focuses on its own problems and needs. As does ITs component selfish organizations or spheres (countries, cultures, collective groups, companies), as do we each from their own perspectives in a negotiated way (i.e., if you are the 'god' of your cells and organs, then look how well you listen to them and treat them compared to how well they treat you).

IT adapts and learns as we learn, as IT builds, creates, and gains knowledge. That knowledge is correlated, synthesized, aggregated, and transmigrated through to the individual's psyche as required (and enhanced or promoted and modified through success and habit).

This then forms part of the individual's collective mind subset (to lesser and greater extents depending on the individual), before being populated across the psyche group (as we sleep, interact, or expose ourselves to the sensationalist media-sphere). A correlated aggregated potentiality of perception and stimulus.

Some memory data elements (symbolism and signifiers) may appear specific to psyche or cultural groups (snakes, writing, symbols, history, beliefs, attitudes, cultural, personality traits, etc.) depending on which cultural sphere you are in. In parallel we learn as individuals, and we do what we think is right or guided to do by love, desire, work, reproduction, thinking, fear, discovering, and try to survive and make the world a better place for us if we can.

At the same time, we are slaves to ourselves collectively, outsmarting and learning from ourselves and adapting to the natural environment (as a process in itself, which by looking at objectively can give perspective on the underlying cause/divine drive).

IT is harsh, feral, an almost artificial AI program in its behaviour, a self-evolving operating system surviving within a server landscape of other competing operating systems within nature (Gaian Bubble).

IT is unforgiving, ruthless, and uses whatever it needs. It does not have the human type emotions we have (as yet). It does not have siblings or peers or parents that it is aware of, or anything it can relate to, or be adjusted to or by (other than the containing global constraints).

So, it has become selfish, moody, demanding, knowledge seeking, controlling, and defensive. IT is, after all, fending for itself in a world in which it is dominant without competition or predator.

So, a balance needs to be struck up between our needs as individuals and IT's needs as a collective entity. We need to get the perspective of the individual balanced with that of the whole. In theory the two should be the same in many respects. It's just that pulling in many directions can cause communication breakdown and loss of obvious joint benefit objectives and cohesion.

This evolutionary process should be working well under perfect conditions and when in balance, where the needs of the one are matched with the needs of the many, in a symbiotic balanced harmonious relationship. But in our case, it is not, not by a long way. There are many things wrong for many reasons on many levels within the collective mind, and externally from an objective perspective to do with latency, legacy, ignorance, physicality, and lack of competition externally, including demographics.

Historical soul structure classes continue competing with one another and old habits die hard. Within this multidimensional virtual-scape of the collective, old biological sourced demonic programs still compete against each other across the human devices.

A sort of hidden landscape or virtual-scape of competing groups of legacy demonic programs at war, all invisibly hidden away from us, but going on inside us and between us all the time (as with 'agents' etc in the Matrix films). All repeating the same battles but with ever more modern scenery.

These 'Angel and Demon' programs inhabiting people with their own agendas, influencing politics, attitudes, direction, and fears. While they are unable to affect the system directly themselves (as they are system derived), they try to influence people, and are drawn or attracted to individuals who have the capability to change the system itself. This can become obvious in crowded places where somehow people (or 'non-player characters') become drawn unconsciously to them. In some cases like busy supermarkets it can be like watching a virtual game of Pacman.

Or theses programs may inhabit people who are associated with individuals they want to influence (angelic individuals), as helpers, guides or guardians. Good or evil.

There is also an invisible naïve residual legacy which affects the 'real' world, although these programs are ancient and outdated. The virtual regressive lag of the REAL gradually aligning with the physical 'real' as it gains cohesion, order and maturity (The Divine Plan).

We 'as devices' are here to learn new things, adapt, perceive, refine knowledge and evolve. We can use the consolidated collective genius knowledge we have hived away, integrate it, enhance and develop it into new ideas and habits via our psyche strata-like structure. It is our knowledge and data built up over time, which has come from us, and is relayed back to us in consolidated ratified form. Yet it cannot grow if we do not learn and add to it.

The New Age concept of simply learning everything from IT (naïvely thinking this is a divine source of knowledge), and being 'at one' with it, and not worrying about self-learning through conventional means, is not what it is all about and very naïve.

We have to do the work and steer our own collective path, and not assume this is 'god-given' inspirational divine knowledge that is somehow already there, and is just being downloaded into *inspired* geniuses gradually over time. Rather than in reality just emerging from the sum of all of our ongoing amalgamated collective thoughts and science.

Although IT has all our knowledge and can correlate information to make assumptions, it does not have our individual human experience or skills or competence.

Such that IT may know everything up to the limits of our understanding of say quantum physics, cybernetics, chemistry, biology, design, etc. to such an extreme degree that it would seem ten years ahead of mainstream understanding.

However, it is stuck, unable to know what to do with it, or how this knowledge fits together to form a worldview perspective, or how to manage it in terms of direction. Think of a thousand Einstein-like geniuses all together in one room, unable to even tie their own shoe laces, or have any understanding of the world outside the window, or what they are meant to be doing, yet wouldn't know how to do it even if they did know (lack of management and political capability).

The individual's psyche is populated with data and functional 'modules' in such a way as to guide a person and influence them in specific ways. This construct provides an interface or interpretation of the collective information pertaining to their role or function (each ant has a specific job).

Yet there is something that controls and influences this psyche element selection process, for some purpose or goal. IT also influences our physical biological structure and functionality – this is why we have two halves to our brain (and other peculiar structuring).

IT sometimes selectively (as a natural process) also allocates specific individuals with roles and functions (character type or preset preprogramed personality types), which has a cause-and-effect stimuli in the same way as at certain times an ant colony selects workers, soldiers, queens, etc. and their functions.

IT is self-regulating, and possibly self-modifying, and yet it is still to be proven capable of self-consciousness beyond the basic childlike awareness that has been encountered through extreme experiences, meaningful mass synchronicity, and mythopoetic traceable media discourse evidence.

Chapter 8
THE LEGACY ISSUES OF OUR COLLECTIVE MIND

IT has evolved many sophisticated control and manipulation systems which are still in place, based on unconscious ignorance, incentives, belief, fear, bribery and needs.

These evolved control structures (established originally as natural behaviours) can manifest themselves in more modern times as religions, technology structures, company groups, cultural boundaries, politics, and traits, and interpersonal relationship protocols.

There can also be external control elements self-introduced to the individuals, e.g., chemicals (vaccines, pills, food additives, hormones), media focus, entertainment forums and parameters, and emotional stimuli and 'suggestion' responses.

At the same time, we individually are growing in numbers, becoming more ignorant, fatter, lazier, blinded by media, suffering newer forms of ill-heath, becoming toxic, inefficient, mentally ill, and unhappy. We are making life hard for ourselves and giving ourselves a raw deal subconsciously, as nothing external is forcing or driving us collectively to be anything else. *We are toxifying ourselves and stagnating.*

When things are not right in a system in nature, errors occur. That is the way nature changes, it adapts and evolves. Errors in the macro-organism – "IT" – can only easily be corrected through external influence, i.e., via a predator, or competition (as normal in nature), or through supply and demand.

Change can also occur periodically by creating its own (or externally stimulated/imposed) point of reference figure (hero individual) that can perceive IT holistically (outside the box) and refine the status-quo (a naturally recurring fault correction subprogram/psyche element – a residual naturally occurring process from nature to promote evolution or change).

Humans have been without any natural competition for tens of thousands of years – long after the dinosaurs lost their kingdom to climate change – but of course they were just stupid and naïve lizards.

It has been so long now that IT has even started *imagining* alien predators for itself as potential threats and 'ancient alien' (lizard like) competition induced by collective fear influencing its child-like dreams and collective active imagination – frightened of what is in the cupboard, and what ITs been watching on TV and reading in magazines, mostly from the 50's, 60's and 70's and sci-fi films.

As a result the system has many legacy software issues ingrained within it from its evolutionary path, with old style mechanisms - or ways of doing things - that are hard to ignore, overcome, or remove (resource gathering, eating, belief structures, fighting, working, travelling, herding, following well-trodden paths, imaginary fears, phobias, traits, habits, and more), along with historical associated data (memory), code latency, and connections (ghosts and such).

Like a planetary Microsoft office suite of programs and Windows operating system, but written lazily and developed by a bunch of naïve idiots with no thought for the future.

In essence, IT has significant amounts of redundant data and program functions within it that would, with competition (or subject to predator incentives), normally be overcome or removed quickly.

In the last century, the collective mind of humanity has also become somewhat corrupted, both in the collective imaginal and the way it 'thinks', because of certain artificial elements entering individual bodies, and affecting individual minds (drugs such as LSD, heavy metals, shamanic 'fungi' practices, toxins, hormones, additives). Especially in certain cultures.

Combined with an overall decline in global and cultural mental health generally, these substances can cause unnaturally invoked peak experiences, or message transfer with corrupted, biased, irrational, or naïve ideas and data coming through the individuals involved (mentioning no names).

This consequently populates the collective database and *'Overmind'* working structure with 'Psychedelic delusions' (wrong perspectives and messages), causing a negative overall feedback effect, thus circumventing and corrupting the natural evolution system process in the past, and introducing 'bad programming' and bad individual worldview data.

This is then reflected back through cultural discourse and influence on society in general (art, media, attitudes, etc.). In an individual, these drugs have the effect of dropping your individual psyche firewall, opening you up to the collective unconscious (uncontrolled and unfiltered) so you can happily go surfing the collective and imaginal in an unrefined manner (exposed to the REAL).

However, opening doors works both ways and this 'opening' also allows collective data and programs to come in and corrupt (hypnotically) your usually well-protected system (think about SPAM, hacking, virus, data corruption, hijacking and various other information systems analogies).

This is especially true for weak-minded individuals, the very young, or those who are easily influenced or open to suggestion. This is also the case with assisted spirituality methods (forced enlightenment techniques) creating links to the collective mind for 'unqualified' (unprepared) individuals, who, in some cases, shouldn't even be trusted to drive a car. These are spiritual surfers who haven't even bothered to learn to swim.

Which is why IT is a mess (*judging by the way it behaves and communicates, by the way we behave and act collectively, and by the naïve ideas within it*).

However, it should be emphasized that IT does not view IT's problems or situation in the same way we do, or with the same objectives. From its perspectives many things are fine to IT, as we are doing what it wants/needs, and IT is unaware things are incorrect or wrong.

IT just does what it does, and what works, and what it can get away with. Which may not be good for us individually, or make it easy to change things. For example, we know drugs are bad for us, but IT may not know any different.

Other forms of spiritual awareness can be achieved through removing left-brained 'ego' layers of immunizing protection, that is, this can be simulated by use of meditation, serious illness or injury requiring resync of blueprint data, a gradual kundalini process, spiritually 'reborn' or reconnected, NDE[23], and as such.

But these are more useful for observational study and analysis of the experience content rather than a means of influencing change in the system.

When we lose consciousness, this simply means losing connection to your mind from physicality (loss of higher peer-to-peer communications 'through the mirror'), allowing safe lower-level communications to occur uninterrupted by conscious interference.

In effect, switching off part of your brain that links to your higher mind (as it were) on a self-awareness basis and also changes in the state of your brain.

As such you no longer are self-aware. You have detached from one paradigm, and now are aware or integrated (locked in) to another that has no time parameters, like a laptop disconnecting from the cloud which is now out of sync and out of contact such that one cannot interconnect and therefore perceive the other on either side.

This allows the brain to reorganize (dream), rest, and then resync. The same process happens also at a collective level, but not as advanced since IT is not as conscious or awake as we are.

---

[23] Lommel, P. V. (2010). *Consciousness beyond life: The science of the near-death experience*. HarperOne.

Chapter 9

WHY CAN'T WE SEE THE WOODS FOR THE TREES

IT subconsciously builds into each individual person and groups a mechanism to disguise itself from them (again, as with ants, it doesn't pay from an evolutionary perspective to know you are a slave in a colony, or be an individual that points out that fact).

People who have experienced IT (this collective entity) seem not even to be allowed to describe it to others, or get their ideas understood. It's as if the obvious concept is always falling on deaf ears, or blind hypnotized vision.

Some of the individuals I have met who have tried to communicate this eventually become hermit-like due to this immunizing ostracizing phenomena, whilst also having to cope with the terrifying repeated extreme exposure of the thing itself, as was the case with Carl Jung.

Also with H. P. Lovecraft, in which he attempts to describe and give discourse context to, via his short stories e.g. The Call of Cthulhu – attempting to articulate a journey to an indescribably powerful, terrifying, and intensely overwhelming entity within a fear inducing dark domain. All derived from his own extreme experiences. Something to which I too can attest.

There is something within every individual's psyche structure that has evolved to be blind and deaf to this obvious situation. In essence, IT hides our collective identity from individuals, and evolves away anyone that tries to point out the reality, or even describe IT, or attempt to remove this cloak of invisibility, whilst manipulating religious structures into blind control structures.

IT is extremely adept at this process of hiding itself from us as individuals, and this is only natural, and necessary for our collective benefit (keeping us part of the herd). Natural selection discourages those who escape the system (truth-seekers) and don't play the game (as outcasts, hermits, seemingly mad, unloved, unhealthy, and undesirable).

IT rewards and promotes those that comply within its boundaries, or conform to its system domain (religious believers, fit, strong, sexy, happy, greedy, smart, the well-integrated), yet even more so those individuals that impose these mass control structural policies and systems on the masses. Even though, ultimately, this may not be in the individual's best interests at heart.

Over time, belief structures change to control structures, with reinforced concepts such as paradise, afterlife, god experience, archetype control, the devil, demons, and angels. Sometimes utilizing previous well established belief symbolism, festivals, and faith structures to help reinforce the believability and number of followers.

These concepts are subconsciously reinforced again via the individual psyche structures through fear, awe, reward, and promised hope (with more up-to-date understanding or the real world).

Yet, the more you try to understand it (the structure, nature, form, and hierarchy) the more complex it becomes in and of itself. If you play the game against IT, IT only improves its own gameplay and methods.

Such that IT is always just one step ahead in this game of chess. After all, IT knows what you are thinking, and you have to think within it and be part of it, or it will react against you with fundamentalist zeal.

As mentioned earlier, each individual has elements and information and processing functionality from the collective unconscious mind within them (to a lesser or greater degree, depending on the individual).

This is appropriate or required pertaining to the group psyche that the individual is part of, and to the role they have (each part forming together to integrate as a whole). The data and functionality within them is of a correlated format (parallel consensus) and is not easily recognizable, or accessible, or contextual to the individual.

Those that have this capability to an extreme level, are either classed as geniuses or mad or enlightened, depending on their role and level of access to the collective and their psyche structure, and where they are socially. This is also dependent on which part of the 'collective elephant in the room' they are experiencing, or connected to part of.

This individual and collective data and parallel knowledge is accessed and updated safely through sleep via the psyche, and through daily interaction with others.

But also, occasionally, through gnosis, which nearly all geniuses have been subject to and yet probably were unaware that this is its term for it (e.g., Wolfgang Pauli, Einstein, Isaac Newton and his metaphysical 'apple' from the tree of knowledge falling on his head).

In reality, gnosis is something that is far more common than people are aware of. It has just been deliberately hidden as a concept due to collective suppression (religiously purged) and by scientific delusion despite many very obvious evidential examples.

Other methods are available to access the data and functionality within the collective unconscious; for example, tools such as kinesiology which uses techniques to access the unconscious subliminally in binary form (Q&A). Or in totality through say cosmic consciousness sometimes generated through 'kundalini awakening' (for want of a better term) with energy activation and the 'twin snakes' of energy rising up the spinal column (which is actually just what it feels like, the sensation of when the nerve elements at each vertebrae (and spinal cord) are activated from the bottom upwards - generating a spiralling feeling and heat energy inside and up the back into the skull - which occurs before data download and interaction collectively occurs with the individual, as represented symbolically as the Caduceus or staff of Hermes.

Anyway, most of these processes are just something very simple going on, and more of a quantum interactive data communication process between the physical (peer levels) and the corresponding *etheric* levels, and not mystical or 'secret' Knights Templar-type mystical or 'dark' knowledge at all.

With this awakening you will become aware of much more going on 'in the world', the corruption, the beguiling media, geopolitical agendas, and bureaucratic mindless institutional controlling systems, and sense a non-existent elite 'them'. Yet you will also be still looking for answers and the bigger truths beyond the fake news, looking for new direction, meaning, and trying to wade through pathways of understanding to make sense of what you have and are experiencing.

It is akin to having been in comfortable 3d cinema all your life, and suddenly finding yourself outside in the rain in a cold busy noisy high street. Abruptly having to deal with the shock of a new vibrant and intense perception of reality (the 'REAL') presented by your senses into your mind. All new and cold and harsh compared to your previously dream-like sheltered oblivious existence.

This new awakened state can be quite overwhelming and difficult to cope with, and the feeling of being lied to and controlled all your life, can be quite depressing. You will have the sense that everyone else is just blind to it, oblivious of what is going on, and you are alone.

However, as you progress up the layers of understanding, and sidestep the constraints and rabbit holes of others, you will increasingly see beyond, and the bigger picture will gradually become clearer as to what is going on, how it works, and how it has all evolved.

This is especially true if you use the work and wisdom of others (especially scientific) who have done the same in the past (rather than latching-on to other non-sensical and irrational interpretations of what you have experienced, shoehorned into some religious or spiritual/alien storyboard).

The scale of and complexity of what you are now confronted with can seem daunting, and it may seem impossible to do anything about it. You may feel you are Surrounded by sleepwalking zombies or even seemingly that you are a different species from those you see about you.

The magnitude and intractability of the system may seem impossible to deal with, and daunting to confront. However, you may be surprised at how easy it is to change things now you are out of the 'matrix' (for want of a better analogy) and seeing it for what it is from both outside, and yet still within it.

From ancient times this sort of awakening or visionary process has been misunderstood, associated with mystical symbolism, witchcraft, and the occult, mostly due to fear and ignorance. It is just a biological process that interfaces to and from a quantum field structure to exchange data.

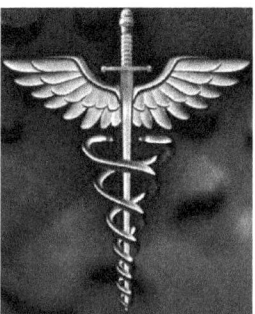

Figure 2. The Caduceus, still in use today

The cosmic consciousness experience, for example, through kundalini, is a process that is also highly unsettling, unnerving, and limits the individual from wanting to discuss the experience or the phenomena or even be able to describe it.

The process does seem to also require an 'other' (as the saying goes, it takes 'two to tango') male and female energy to make it work effectively or to influence/interact, a sort of two-person rule. Both of whom have to be highly interactive to and of the collective information system. (people who are interactive with IT and not just passive observers of the phenomena and 'spiritual' mysticism).

There has been a lot of rubbish written about this 'kundalini' awakening process, mostly from an Eastern naïve cultural symbolism understanding, which can be disregarded. It is just an evolved biological process for data transfer to and from the etheric, and as a result has successfully avoided significant scientific study and analysis due to its stigma and poor interpretation by naïve individuals.

This process occurs naturally before birth (an *informing* process to the body and mind) when the inner spinal cord canal channel is open, which interfaces directly to the etheric body blueprint within the Pleroma, a *channel* that becomes closed during and shortly after birth.

With other types of spinal cord stimulation it can be seen that the nerves in the spine cause electrical signal energy to flow up into the brain and stimulation of the brain stem, hypothalamus, pineal, and temporal lobes inducing effects such as Déjà Rêvé – mass dream recollection and loss of awareness. Again I have extensive experience of this phenomena, and have been involved with many experiments involving scans and EEG sensor stimulus and diagnostics etc. In essence this is a stimulation of a natural process (one that exists for the unborn and small babies as a learning/exposure process until it is ceased when the central spial canal closes) and only reactivated during stress or crisis or need or stimulation when much older.

In effect this is simulating a mental focal seizure in similar form to mild epilepsy but in a controlled manner. In the case of Déjà Rêvé this has the effect of forcing previously hidden unconscious dreams, memories and thoughts to the conscious mind at once, while still maintaining physical coordination.

The particular Déjà Rêvé experience we are interested in here (rather than the other types) is where complex dreams (vivid or otherwise) and thoughts over the last few months come flooding back combining together, and suddenly making perfect sense and clarity, and with full recollection in conscious awareness with meaning feeling and emotions, and sequence (even timings of the original dreams), combined with gnosis.

All presented in the form of some unconscious dialogue or 'conversation' at the unconscious level. However (in my experience of these events) in most cases this is not particularly useful or does not have any logical or rational meaning or value or rationale. Still in around 5% of the time it can lead to an indication of a dialogue or flow of ideas with the collective mind.

Experiments to simulate effect and process using electrical stimulation have generated similar results but further research has been considered potentially harmful, and not least highly unsettling and exhausting.

In general when communication occurs, data transferred to and from the physical to the *etheric* in every case is constructed in a piece (encoded packet) or encoded data block form (as with peer-to peer communications), and combined together and linked into flows of data back and forth.

Once processed, this collective knowledge is then ordered (compartmentalized) into themes or knowledge disciplines such as quantum mechanics, biology, and chemistry, in a similar way to modern distributed database networks, which in themselves happen to emulate natural biological processes.

The collective data transmitted is held and managed (correlated/aggregated/consolidated) efficiently within the quantum information field structure (etheric knowledge base), although most of it is not useful to the individual device (person) in terms of productivity.

It is a growing correlated synthesized amalgamation of our collective humanitarian knowledge and thoughts (aka Akashic records). However, in some cases the data itself has become misguided, inconsistent, biased, and quite often just wrong. (Unlike, of course, the Internet) ☺.

The direction for populating (prioritizing) this knowledge acquisition is influenced by the collective mind itself, and managed into stovepipes (subjects or topics akin to academic domains or fields of study).

Individuals are guided down these paths, drawn to specialties or fields of learning, to 'success' or finding answers or expanding the understanding regardless of their overall use, purpose, or benefit.

Chapter 10
STRUCTURE AND FORM OF THE COLLECTIVE MIND

The scale of influence of the collective mind structure functionality increases from the bottom up (stratified). The animalistic subconscious or base elements have priority, and are very strong (established over a long period of time over millions of years).

The higher 'unconscious' elements or functions are passive (subliminal/hypnotic) but still highly influential.

However, the more recent 'conscious' functions/influence and data structures are very subtle, sporadic, unpredictable, and limited in effect and influence (similar to our own depth psyche structure but without as much conscious influence).

Although the speed of effect is inversely proportional, conscious changes take at least a few weeks (or much longer) in some cases to manifest (enter the system) or be discoursed.

Global psyche group cultures (for example, Asian, European, American, and their sub organizations) form groups (component parts – organisms) within the collective and subgroups (like multiple arms of an octopus) which are subsumed when they are perceived/associated together as one whole.

Some are more advanced (intellectually, mentally, knowledge base, influence – mental age) than others, which encourages cross mixing between cultures and 'bullying' from one to another (although the more self-proclaimed "advanced" cultures may not necessarily be going in the right direction).

We need to develop a managed programme of conscious change for this playful yet terrifying collective octopus with its several cultural tentacles and collective landscape of archetypal controlling and conspiring subconscious array of hierarchical demonic/angelic programs controlling IT and us.

Figure 3. You are here – avoid being a sucker

As mentioned earlier IT seems to have a level of mental maturity (based on evidence of its behaviour) to that of a very young child (baby octopus). In effect, it has the energy and knowledge of ten thousand football stadiums but the mindset and behavioural maturity of a supra-genius five-year-old girl.

IT's mental maturity is behind us as individuals and our level of conscious awareness. Just in the same way that an AI program can never be as wise as its programmers – even though it may be impressively intelligent (similarly cells in the body are very clever, sophisticated, and smart, and we could never do or understand what they do).

IT is like a child genius that knows everything, but has not yet developed responsibility, mature attitudes, or disciplines and adult behaviour. IT is brilliant and awe inspiring to behold, but you wouldn't let it drive your car (which of course IT can't, as it can't reach the pedals ☺).

IT has inverse characteristics (data mapping, and data format) to us, which is a consequence of the diametric nature of the relationship (as with us and our cells). Therefore, from our perspective, IT seems to reward bad behaviour, and conversely, if you try and help IT, IT can have the opposite effect.

The bottom-line is don't treat it like a rational logical human child requiring parenting or schooling (or sibling influence). IT has to be managed and instructed, and sometimes bribed.

Although I wouldn't suggest *spare the rod and spoil the child* as a suitable idiom, especially if you are the one found holding the rod/staff.

IT has no concept of time, as you would expect from any operating program in a virtual state machine, with time having no meaning or context (time is something we humans have created in our minds to make sense of reality).

'We' are its body and mind, but it does not see or understand the concept of physical reality as we do, or feel or think as we do, and its priorities and perspectives are very different (chaos, probable futures, vortex data flows, energy patterns).

So, it is aware of future probabilities (Woodcock, 2021) which seem real to IT (whereas to us are unknowable, and

Influencing the Collective Unconscious Mind

only in potential) but can be discoursed to individuals through precognitive or projection visons.

IT is the cause of fate and destiny for us, and IT is, in effect, just a giant conspiracy, with us all as the conspirators.

In some larger *demonic*-driven conspiracies these are in effect acting independently like some collective psychosis (psychosis being the key concept) as a functioning trans-human collective program acting partly independently, and also hiding itself away, and acting independently from the main (as with a psychosis in the individual).

In these instances, this collective sub-program is serving in some naïve unconscious manner according to its own rules and methods of existence.

It perpetuates doing what it thinks it is supposed to be doing from its own limited objective understanding, ancient legacy programming, and compartmentalized mission and rules. This, in turn, can also be influenced by other collective psychosis *demonic* program conspiracy agenda archon groups, interworking to meet their own naïve unconscious serving program of mass population control or media manipulation.

They even play games with each other in conspiracy and counter conspiracy agendas, all of which seem totally irrational to the powerless logical human.

IT is also very self-interested and curious of its environment. That is a component in its nature, to protect itself and survive, but this then tends it to highlight or focus on problems (problems that we focus on and give energy to in the media such as errors, disasters, catastrophes) rather than its own 'health/fitness' and future.

The sensationalist media-sphere within IT is operating essentially in what is characterized by some as a 'female' manner (which, for IT, includes gossip, emotional intelligence, obsessional, bitchy, drama, catastrophizing and looking for worst case scenario, creating and feeding chaos, promoting de-masculinization and impotence, reducing fertility, tall male poppy syndrome, and emotional fearmongering). Yet leaving the young men players confused, inactive, lost and un-empowered, and the young women players unstable, anxious, chaotic and insecure – in a cyclic negative feedback loop.

Chapter 11
WHAT IS 'IT' INFLUENCED BY?

IT is influenced by, and associates with, 'heavenly bodies' (the moon, sun, stars), both physically via the perception of human devices and subjectively by reinforced concepts created by the devices ("us").

This can be linked to physical perception of moon phases, day/night, planetary positions, seasons, which leads to things like astrology and star sign character attribution, which is valid yet self-fulfilling. Now, this may well be just in relation to our human obsession/fixation with those things that we can see 'in the heavens'. But there is also a real relation to the earthly annual cycle, effectively imposed on IT by phase changes within the Gaian server, i.e., IT produces different sorts of human 'ant' personality types with archetypal templates at different times. So, there really is something valid behind concepts such as astrology (who knew, eh?).

As pointed out and important to recognize - IT cannot affect the physical world except via the devices (physical individuals) or by itself influencing the Gaian operating system and global server in extreme cases, sort of summoning or instigating parental intervention within the *noosphere* which happens very rarely.

IT will not help you individually, as it does not know how from its non-physical virtual reality. Remember IT is hard minded, sometimes brutally selfish, and self-interested, and often bureaucratic. That is what it has learnt to be, while *we* have become soft and easily manipulated. But we still have to live together (IT and us) and get along with each other.

There are many factors influencing, controlling, directing this global collective human 'hive' mind (IT).

There are physical rules and boundaries, constraints, laws, limits, direction, 'a swinging pendulum', spin, rhythm, atomic parameters and dimensional frameworks, constants, chaos, cycles, phenomenology, and so forth (both physical and within the unified filed).

All these factors and elements govern or drive "IT" and us in a 'divine-ward' direction, i.e., in different subtle ways from the bottom up that shape how the collective programs within IT are written, modified, bound, and formed ('The Word', a sort of language structure).

Somehow, IT makes sense out of this, 'divine' way, and evolves into and within it or 'by' it. The 'software' expanding within the constraints and rules of the planetary and universal hardware and firmware, which gives more weight to the notion of an external yet absent universal 'creator' that generated this cosmic 'egg' universe, and consequently our galaxy and planet earth, in this way.

As mentioned earlier, IT is contained within, and has developed from a supporting, sustaining, and driving subsystem (planetary firmware, hardware, DNA template bios). It adheres to patterns constrained by matter, laws of the universe, gravity, energy, sub atomics, DNA, electromagnetics, harmonics and communicates through set frequency bands (scales/keys and/or pitch) to bandwidth limits.

In effect, it has morphic habits, and uses matter memory capacity (physical to quantum field data linkage on a hierarchical level basis).

This field-based information system and data structure projects data into physicality through resonance at specific harmonic peer-to-peer frequencies (including thoughts at the higher levels – synchronization). The more complex exchanges of higher-level data require more time to percolate. Human thoughts exchange data over milliseconds rather than nanoseconds for cells, whereas thoughts within our collective mind – IT – can take weeks.

IT is also affected by other co-existing 'operating systems' supporting other species subsets (less developed pack/herd animal types such as dogs, horses, dolphins, and so forth), all coexisting in one competitive eco DNA information subsystem. All cohabiting and contained inside a planetary field based 'server' capable of supporting multiple programs, operating systems, and evolving bio diverse devices within an integrated competing distributed entangled network.

All of which is constrained and directed by a rule-set providing description, and a functional directional purpose. For example, dominant psyche collective groups within IT – and within this global natural (Gaian) system – will attempt to subsume and dominate weaker ones. It's a rule of nature – just ask a Dodo.

Also, individual devices (people) are capable of interacting and bonding with devices from other high-level collective species (again, such as dogs, cats, horses, apes, dolphins and so forth) with the capability of information transfer, and shared perceptions (not just at the physical level) (as studied by Rupert Sheldrake) [24]. It is an intelligence agency dealing in knowledge, all of which is

---

[24] Sheldrake, R. (1758/2012). *The Science Delusion*. Coronet Books.

managed on a 'need to know' basis, the data stored within its agents as an overall information system.

As far as emulating this system with technology and science (and media), we are still hundreds of years away from successfully emulating this collective mind (IT's operation, architecture, processes, data-form and speed of processing, structure) using software and quantum computing models and AI systems.

We are also a long way from replicating the field-based information system that supports it by using computer hardware. We have taken many millennia to biologically and naturally evolve and develop this system with its highly complex intricacy and sophisticated adaptation. Natural selection has refined its structure, knowledge, information flow, and protection mechanisms. So, even the latest advances in theory for AI and robotic self-awareness, quantum computing and super-cooled fractal crystal data storage are still a long way from emulating IT, and the vast data environment it exists in or being able to simulate it or even provide an effective analogy.

Yet everything we develop is actually being driven in that direction. Technology in the physical world is being driven to be ever more an emulation and simulacra of IT, and the way the unified field operates. Virtual scenery, architecture, crypto currencies, assets, trade, social interaction, images, commerce, clubs and real estate. Yet still with many physical world rules and constraints, and conversely emulating the real physical world in virtual-scapes, and all the trappings.

Yet the physical world technology we have developed is a poor copy of the speed of data flow, memory capacity and vast data storage that exists within the quantum field information structure.

Understand that we (as individual and collective physical humans) are a global network of highly interactive and refined biological quantum computers, installed with hierarchical archetypal programs, and as such we are also acting as a network of devices which also form collective cultural organs.

We as IT (a body without organs) are a humanity-driven information technological singularity within a *'Gaian operating system and global server'*. As such, we can also use that technology to emulate parts of its operation and function (using say virtual role-playing games, Internet, collaborative working practices), and as such consciously use those systems and mechanisms to influence IT.

The architecture of IT is formed more like a structured blueprint or guided framework built on different levels (parts within parts, bubbles within bubbles, within a sphere). It is almost as if IT is developing into something else on-going that is only partly-built, a construction underway of which we have just formed the lower-level building blocks.

It would appear that there are templates for eventual higher levels for this collective entity, but we have not properly populated these – we have not evolved enough as yet to become more than we can be – and spent too much energy on the lower levels such that our collective is still too regressively developed and evolved.

This Macro-Organism/Overmind can only change with external influence; otherwise, it will stay within its evolutionary niche, wherein it will just mutate, toxify, and evolve without direction, using up the resources within its global container and stagnating.

As with Peter Schloderdik's bubbles and foam philosophical concept model[24], IT is contained within the Gaian global hierarchical consciousness structure sphere, both physically and in a virtual quantum field based joined consciousness. A sort or Russian doll idea.

This is also rather like the concept of the Gnostic *demiurge* and Sophia, with IT being the demiurge and Sophia being Gaia or the planetary bubble or matrix 'goddess', the one being a subset of and within, and having been generated by the other.

Our individual egos operate as individual immunizing bubble-like defensive layering systems. These systems protect us from the 'REAL' and unfriendly depths of the void, and also the extreme and sometimes aggressive nature of data and programs in the collective unconscious.

Equally, the collective ego and cultures within our collective mind (IT) also form themselves into the same protecting immunizing bubbles (belief and control structures) from other elements in the Gaian bubble (nature). Protecting itself and its 'organs' from danger.

Like a ship in the water safe from the raging stormy sea and attack from other shipping and sea monsters from the void below – and all the while changing from a basic exploratory Kon-Tiki raft, to a fishing boat, to a yacht, to a battleship - or in our case - an oversized, lazy, decadent four-funnelled complacent cruise liner.

IT, however – although being 'smaller', with less 'capacity' and contained within this global consciousness Gaian sphere and physical world field bubble, IT is more mature/evolved/self-aware than the larger.

In effect, our human *collective consciousness demiurge entity* is more advanced and mature than its *earth goddess Sophia mother* - I am using analogy and symbolism here – there is no actual 'goddess' it is just a metaphor.

I also believe this is the case on a scaling level, with ever *inversely* increasing levels of 'maturity' in that the galactic, or universal consciousness is something that has to be grown within or expanded *into* both physically and expanding or higher levels of consciousness.

In effect, IT is an ever evolving and growing 'GOD', a universal consciousness 'in potential', the universal consciousness being much in the same concept as a cosmic egg. With the universe (or rather the universal unified field combined with the physical universe) template being generated by an external (absent) 'creator' that has no involvement other than at the very lowest preconfigured level (laws, structure, physics, nature and such).

Again, though this has been derived from gnosis, it does seem to align with more recent philosophical and scientific opinion.

Chapter 12

THE WAY FORWARD

So, IT is not 'god', IT just thinks it is (and is very good at persuading people that it is, and becoming ever more adept at reinforcing that delusion).

IT did not create the universe, or this planet. We have created IT, not the other way around.

IT is, though, ever more 'aspiring to become one', growing, learning, controlling, evolving, and adapting, eventually over-coding the planet, system, galaxy and universe. (that after all is the whole purpose, the reason we are here, to expand and evolve consciousness).

Which it will fail to do unless it becomes more awake/self-aware, and learns to resolve its shortcomings on its own.

In order to do this, we need to shake off the collective human mind dominance – change the old *demiurge* form, and old archetypal model forms. We also need to reconnect with the natural Gaian planetary consciousness and allow refinement of IT through our connection to nature, reconnecting to the source data and patterning.

In so doing, we are maintaining that link, that connection, rather than being blocked by IT from our natural environmental roots, and consequently Itself, i.e., we need to avoid *'going Borg'* (as in the Star Trek films).

We need to get back that vital energy, that zest for life, that shining light in our eyes that has been replaced by dull lifeless electronic *Truman Show* emptiness.

We can each do this individually by reconnecting to nature, resyncing, harmonizing, listening, becoming part of it again – rejecting cities, becoming more nomadic, losing the resource grabbing hive-like tendencies, freeing ourselves from control structures.

None of which is easy. We need to wake up to what is going on, and avoid being kept blind to our natural environment by and from ourselves. Or, at least, achieve a holistic balance between the two agendas and paradigms. We need to learn, become more intelligent, and adapt more efficient *ways of being* both individually and collectively.

Equally, we need to appreciate that IT does not 'think' or behave or react in the same way that we do. IT's nature (size, scope, objectives, awareness and so forth) is different, and you cannot apply the same comparatives or analogies to IT as we would to each other as individuals, that is, personality, nature, and attitudes.

IT is made from thought forms and knowledge but aggregated, and these collective thought forms and knowledge perspectives, which in themselves have logical paradoxes, may seem to us as irrational. IT is, after all, a life form in and of itself, of which we are components (as specks of water in the 'Myst' of consciousness, each with an individual fractal perspective of a timeless alternate paradigm, and interacting as one in an interconnected, swarming murmuration, or in our case a bunch of flockers).

IT is not in our image or 'like us' in many regards. IT is more 'dragon like' or animalistic and defensive in nature, or sometimes behaving as a very young female child with its response and stereotype behaviour. As can be seen to its response to a male 'hero' change agent. But IT should not be confused as being in any way human-like, or thought to react and behave in the same way, or to be treated as such.

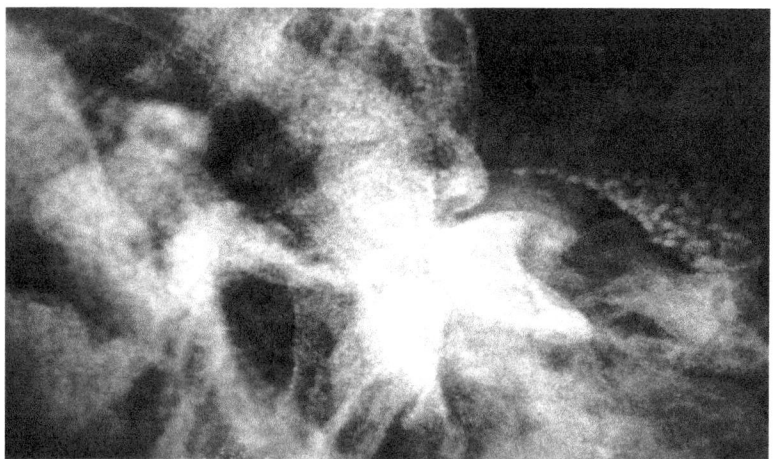

Figure 4. The Myst of Consciousness
Source: Bennet & Bennet, 2020[25]

IT certainly doesn't have a beard and sit on a giant throne on the top of a mountain – yes, it's a bit of a let-down I know, and it isn't what you were expecting – but we have created this thing collectively, and we have nothing to blame but ourselves for its creation.

So, we just have to make the best of IT. Equally, now we know we can consciously change or reprogram this blind collective unconscious entity ourselves (slowly and carefully). IT won't and can't do it by ITtself.

The alternative is to let it fall again (as with the repeating cycle of rise and fall of civilisations) which again is a natural process. A process that many feel will happen anyway. With a new possibly better version emerging from the ashes.

---

[25] Bennet, A., & Bennet, D. (2020). Patterns in the Myst: Messages from the universe. MQIPress.

Chapter 13

How TO INFLUENCE 'IT'

A Guide to Some Methods, Techniques and Objectives

Once there is a clearer picture in your mind of what you are dealing with here i.e. what IT is, being conscious of IT. In theory you should then be able to influence IT (rather than being blind to it and a zombie slave unable to do anything). Which is all very well until you realise what is involved and the dangers.

In theory if you are able to influence it you should also look for the measurable effects, rather than just being an observational and passive observer to the phenomena as it disappears over the edge.

One of the key factors to take into account is that you are - in effect - playing the part of a conscious actor in the hero journey play or game. You are in essence following a script, and it is possible to change that script, to influence IT's response (programming an AI system reaction). You have to edit the play, modify the game software and gameplay – you can't just stop everything and start from scratch.

You can influence the script that others are following by influencing the collective human mind through techniques such as mythopoesis (creative modernization of the hero journey).

There are many other ways of influencing change such as invoking cosmic consciousness feedback, or stimulating meaningful synchronicity, and also through using other *spiritual* techniques to discover what is going on within the system (what is being registered or picked up on), and measuring response through cultural media-sphere discourse such as the news.

But in effect all you can do is make very minor and subtle changes - like nudging the wheel of the Titanic. By applying 'real world' conscious visibility rather than being drawn into the collective unconscious virtual-scape of 'ancient aliens' archetypes, visionary hypnotic influences and illogical childish irrational virtual illusional collective imaginal storylines.

Our collective mind (like a thousand football stadiums) is somewhat child-like and repetitive, and all you can do is maybe change the beat of a drum, or flash a sign up on the billboards, and see if anything happens.

Indicators of Change

One of the key indicators of change happening – as Carl Jung[28] in his works, and from his more recently published Red Book[26], was so interested in – is if you notice an increased intensity of stimulated focused and directed synchronistic events happening around you.

These events may also coincide with a correlation with meaning of those events in relation to the subject you are focusing on (relating to topic). As if the focus is a sort of conversation with the synchronistic events having a meaning, flow and context.

With more people involved, we should see much more coordinated change (i.e., with more blue and black butterflies all nudging the wheel of the Titanic at once in the same

---

[26] Jung, C (2010) *The red book – Liber novus.* Norton Publishing

direction) creating an effective high-level 'Maharishi Effect', coherence and positivity that influences the larger natural and/or social environment.

With more concentration, the process itself should generate synchronous events within the working group itself (reflected back at them and 'on-topic'), and in the content (subject and nature) of subsequent cultural media discourse of things happening *in the world*.

Simple conscious input into the unconscious system can make a big difference if done correctly and in a timely manner. Many people in the past would have been unaware of the changes they were making as it takes quite a time to be processed (percolate through the system) and then for feedback to occur.

Equally, they would not have been aware of the possibility of this phenomena or know what to look for.

Yet, you should never underestimate the power and effect of individual true conscious thought and intention when passed into the collective unconscious mind (despite it seeming impossible and too large a problem to do anything about). It has effects that are sometimes not obvious, and can take some time to be seen, but which can be very dramatic and alarming if you are not prepared.

Thus, it can be very surprising what dramatic change a small amount of this conscious intervention can have on the unconscious zombie land Titanic.

With modern technology and rapid media response, we should now go way beyond the capability of a naïve '*Hero with a thousand faces*' individual (as described by Joseph Campbell)[1], and develop a concerted coordinated group effort to a managed plan, adopting practical refined working methods rather than theoretical approaches. Developing techniques for effecting those changes and measuring them, in a managed form, with effective monitoring processes outside any political arena.

In the modern era, it is much easier to detect changes and see responses happening in news and electronic media platforms, and other forms of media discourse, e.g., films). Such as *The Matrix Resurrections - Lana Wachowski* – which from the trailers seem to have an alarming number of commonalities and synchronicity of events and scenes – 'Neo and Trinity' handshake, blue-black butterflies, starling numerations, city street matrix, mirror of consciousness, the lift, thinking in the bath with a duck on his head, psychologist interview, and Trinity "waiting my whole life for you".

Thousands of years ago the same effect could take decades to percolate (through say art and writing and events), and where the only form of news or communication was word of mouth.

Also, when an individual has many progressive peak esoteric experiences (a sort of psycharcheology) and as is normally the case that individual is driven or compelled to write it down or express it in some form.

They subsequently include their own imaginative constructs to describe those experiences, revamping the original symbols objects story Mythos (mythopoesis) that they grew up with or have been exposed to unconsciously.

It is important to get this recorded somehow (and dated) but also in genuine form (i.e., what they *actually* experienced, described as best as possible, rather than their own mythopoetic creation. The raw experience data is needed as part of the process. Keep a journal.

The Transfer of Data

During this process, the connection (transfer of data) between the individual and the collective will subsequently be picked up on (perceived or channelled) by other sensate types, and then reinforced or reimagined, then in turn given energy and further form by them.

This occurs especially if this has been written down in physical form, as has happened throughout history as with say *The Bible*, so people can read it and reimagine, connect to, and regenerate the story. It is that 'magic spell' writing or 'Magik Book' creation that hypnotically keeps the Mythos alive.

Subsequently, the individuals who merely channel (read only) visionaries, out-of-body experiencers, vivid dreamers, shamanic practitioners, etc., do not influence the collective mind in themselves but provide very useful (reader) information as to what is going on within it (what IT has received).

Consequently, in current times it is a good idea to keep an eye on the online conversations of these 'channelling' groups (e.g., ancient alien religious followers) to see what they are currently discussing online, and also the *level* of stimulation – how busy they are. See if the subject matter includes themes, events, or a change in story direction.

Work out what it really relates to in both world event terms, and what is being done through mythopoesis, and what is happening to these real physical 'Hero Journey' role-playing characters who are (unaware in most cases – inadvertent 'illuminati') changing the script and realigning the virtual scenery (see A Kazlev)[8].

From an author's viewpoint, there appears to be a strong correlation in subject and timing to many aspects of what has been written in the author's published fictional books, (see Additional Reading section at the end) to what appears in these discussion groups in subject, intensity, and concepts. Along with the media reporting of news events and illogical focus.

Choosing Topics to Influence IT

In terms of choosing topics to influence the collective, it should be emphasized – and so we repeat it here – that *IT gets bored easily, or with subjects or things that become tricky, and then moves to the next interesting thing.*

You have to keep it interested with games and toys. Be Action Man or Barbie, be a new gadget, energetic, novel and exciting. Also, hide things from it playfully, come up with new and exciting things and ideas.

You have to play outsmarting games with the dragon (with an underlying influential direction), and stay competitive. Yet do this carefully – always remembering you are a butterfly in the eye of a storm, so it is advisable not to get carried away – you are playing with fire – literally.

As such, it should also be emphasized that there is quite an element of danger involved. Exposure to the 'fullness' of the collective mind can be dangerous and terrifying, as can the process of attempting to influence it.

Opening your mind to the REAL and its extreme numinous intensity and physical effects, is much the same as taking your virtual RPG gameplay headset off and sticking your head into a nuclear reactor core, combined with processing the data flow of a mainframe quantum computer in your head.

Once done it takes up to at least two weeks for the conscious prepared concept thought projected through cosmic consciousness (into the void, or using mythopoesis to percolate through the system, to be processed and thought-formed into a reflected response.

This will appear in the physical world as cultural discourse, channelled through individual's visions, vivid dreams, gnosis and translated through and into inspirational art (art, music, media-sphere, performance arts, books, social media, etc.). This process only works, though, when IT is actively engaged or involved with something, again, like a child that is focused on a game or a toy.

You can only get IT to do something or think of something that relates to the game or story or toy (some form of association), otherwise, it just isn't interested in it and there is no effect (no relative response).

As stated earlier, the response to this programming can also be reflected back in the form of news events or reports on the very subject you were thinking about, not just in terms of the topic, but using your actual words and thoughts.

An echo of the very same idea, the same locations and scenario, with this echo taken from an idea and manifested into reality as actionable change in the status quo of reality – people getting your thoughts and ideas and acting on them. The author has documented dozens of examples taken with physical evidence of this phenomena happening over the last 15 years, to a degree that is unquestionable and evidential, and some of these have been documented in his fictional books (see Additional Reading section at the end).

Preparing for the Process

If you are going to attempt this process (if that is you have a choice), it helps being healthy, fit, and having good energy. You will need to be psychologically strong and balanced, and generally in a quiet environment free from distraction, demands, interruptions and external environmental interference, e.g., EMF interference Wi-Fi, LED lighting, 5G, etc.

Also, being physically free from illness and chemicals, toxins, heavy metals, drugs, and having balanced energy and good vitality seems to help. In some cases, though, certain drugs such as DMT, Psilocybin, or Ayahuasca can be useful to gain access and explore and perform psycharcheology.

However, although the author has not used these (and doesn't recommend them), there is no evidence they are effective in influencing the collective mind in any constructive way, and in extreme cases could affect IT in adverse ways, with the consequences having a negative effect on the collective mind as well as the individual mind and body.

It is well known that certain drugs facilitate access to different levels and natures of spiritual experiences as they operate, integrate, or channel through 'the mirror' at different molecular or set biological frequencies/bands (ref Erik Davis, P K Dick, Terrence and Dennis McKenna[27]; H P Lovecraft). They gain access (in effect) to different sections or domains of the imaginal parts of the collective human mind strata (different domains/sections/aspects/strata).

---

[27] McKennas, Dennis and Terrence (2012) *The brotherhood of the screaming abyss.*

Which also accounts for the different forms of esoteric experience and the nature and content of the data in each case. NDEs (near death experiences) interface to a different context of the collective mind as opposed to say visions (individual or group) which interact with/to the collective imaginal virtual dreamscape, vivid dreams, spiritual encounters, or certain peak experiences.

However, not enough scientific work and calculated experimentation has been done in this area; it has been somewhat random and historically irresponsible.

Sensing Interaction with IT

This is a long slow process and you will not be immediately aware of anything happening, especially with mythopoeic writing, which is a form of 'magic craft' or *Magik* and requires practice. Putting information and ideas into the system though thought and writing and visionary interaction and gnosis all take time to percolate through.

Mythopoesis can also only have an effect if it is interactive, i.e., the story is received through you (via visions, channelling, gnosis, etc.) and then modified by you, then written down (something physical that can be read – it doesn't need to be handwritten but does need to be printed physically). Then reinvented using an adaptation of an existing construct that is already built within the imaginal as a story.

The modification and enhancements and the interpretation or perception of the way things are in the physical world now, are then channelled into something new (e.g., ancient myth becomes sci-fi), and modernized not only in techo-scenery but in script, technology, scientific concepts, and storyline. The one following the other through mythopoesis and imagination, and then the story and images and ideas being echoed or reflected back through visions -ancient aliens, UFOs, trans-dimensional beings etc.

In effect, it is like receiving the dream of a child and then helping to shape that dream in a meaningful conscious direction (re-imagining it), only modernizing it so it is more acceptable and reasonable, believable, and more in line with physical reality and knowledge and understanding.

This allows the dream to grow rather than continue to repeat the same repetitive unconscious dream resolution process, dream loops, and the 'been here before' cycles.

But the process has to be involved with the live intent and activity of the collective mind. It has to be interesting, activating the imagination, and fun. Even humorous, as humour tends to help break down communication barriers between individuals (brain cells in the collective mind), and implies a measure of safety.

But you have to be 'in the game', one of the 'hero action figures' on the board of the archon 'gods' (which are all as one). Even if you are in the game and you are say 'fighting the dragon', you will lose, but you have the option of losing in a certain direction, (fighting the dragon on the back foot, sword and shield in hand, as you back up across the high flimsy wooden bridge).

In these instances (or when it is happening), there will be a feeling of intensity in the air, a sense of energy of 'something going on' and a state of being that you are interconnected with others.

A sort of 'buzz' or frequency of energy or something having a higher interest in you – *an immanence or presence.*

Many people have referred to this approaching feeling of immanence in varied descriptive ways. An awareness of something else there and present. We are not talking about an individual presence (psychology related, psychosis, or shadow self) but here more of a 'divine' presence as experienced during the South Pacific atomic bomb testing, PKD, McKennas in La Chorrera, Constantine leaving Rome and the collective vision, and various recorded religious collective 'divine presence' events. This experience can be highly intimidating and overwhelming, but hopefully – once you understand what is actually happening – it will become less so over time. But still, don't forget your Teddy ☺.

You can also become sensitive to (aware of) collective world events happening just *before* they occur, and more so as they are happening somewhere (disasters, terror attacks, catastrophes, riots, and collective entity events of focus where many people are afraid, excited or become emotional at once together, e.g., 9/11). Specifically, also events that IT is interested or involved in. These will then be highlighted in the news and media shortly after.

IT can also stimulate quantum perturbations in the noosphere - quantum field variance or non-random fluctuation - which can be detected electronically as variations in the random quantum fields such as those identified in the Global Consciousness Project (see Dean Radin)[10], Which are, in effect, certain events causing increased activity in the collective operating system which result in measurable effects in the global quantum field 'server'.

The author has directly been sensitive to many of these fluctuations and key events, and has recorded evidence. Many of these events have been related to activity and events specifically known to have been happening involving the collective human mind, and followed up with associated media reporting. A few it would appear that the author may have ultimately been responsible for and documented.

IT in turn is also affected/agitated by global gravitational field variance (earthquakes, eruptions etc.) as well as celestial gravitation variance from planets to some extent, although this may be more habitual/psychological/habit formed rather than practical/real. But more so, moon and solar orbital gravitational variance and anomalies, as per star signs. So, IT may only be receptive or active (or awake) at certain times or phases – and that may correspond with a feeling of energy of something happening 'in the air'.

However, it is not just an annual variance pattern that IT follows. There are various cyclic pattern maps derived by spiritualist groups which attempt to predict how this sequence varies. There are several cycles involved – a bit like biorhythms for an individual person, but collectively and on a much longer timeframe and more complex. However, again this may be more reactive (collective psychosomatic) rather than adhering to any specific real pattern. But there are phases when IT seems asleep and other times when IT is very much awake, active, and responsive.

When 'something is going on' or you are 'doing something', there will generally be aching from the crown chakra (for want of a better term – the soft spot on the top of the head). An intense heat and strong ache on the top of the skull in a circle just smaller than your palm, penetrating several centimetres into the skull.

This energy does not appear on any MRI scan, CT scan, or EEG brain sensor scans (the author has spoken with neurosurgeons and neurologists and had these scans done), but there is definitely a localized detectable measurable heat, energy, and sensation that is there. At times it can feel very intense, like a solid rod extending a few inches into the skull and out the top of the head, and is pivotal backwards and forwards. This condition generally coincides with gnosis events (downloads – information coming in or something collectively going on in the world such as a terror attack or collective fear or stress, or if you are concentrating on some subject or situation – i.e., doing something).

Staying Spiritually Awake and Active

You need to be spiritually awake, aligned, focused and able to outsmart IT if need be, to see past its hypnotic imagination, and be a player in the hero story game, an action figure character in the Jason and the Argonauts god interactive virtual role-playing Dungeons and Dragons board game. As you play, the set of role-playing game rules grows, and adapts over time as needed, although not very quickly.

So, if these intentions or actions are having an effect, you will notice (especially if working with a group) significant increases in the number and frequency and intensity of synchronistic events (noticeable synchronicity, not just coincidences). The nature of them (nature, topic, those involved, subject) can form a meaningful mechanism of communication on the subject matter in question. This can be on the order of several *Jungian beetle* type synchronicities a day with some common meaning or theme. But this can sometimes be very hard to get to the bottom of, and record, or work out the association – it requires a lot of detective work and it is good to remain very sceptical.

When trying to invoke change, it is important to focus on specific ideas or topics (particularly using keywords, e.g., 'sustainability' or on a country or topic, and relate these keywords to a picture or concept (the word and the action). That keyword concept should then (after it has percolated through the system) start to appear (be reflected back in terms of sensationalized media reporting, news reports appearing suddenly on the very subject in question) or discourse.

You may notice a sudden switch or refocusing in the topics of subjects people are talking about, and the focus of governments, etc. In essence, this process is giving IT ideas in the form of NLP (neurolinguistic programming). The process seems to work in the same way information systems have tokens or signifiers, adjusting the AI code of an android so that it is more inclined to think and talk and be directed to act along certain subject paths (as with Jiminy Cricket to Pinocchio).

Remember, *IT is us and we are IT* – we are part of IT and *IT is NOT A SEPARATE ENTITY* from us individually.

We are like integrated brain cells within IT, and interconnected together (one system). But we all have differing agendas and objectives and perspectives from each other, and from IT as a collective entity. It is important to keep remembering this; don't start thinking of it as an adversary or something else alien to you. Parts of this collective brain and body work differently, and do different things, but the brain itself also operates as a whole.

IT exists both within the field-based etheric Pleroma and within its component physical devices in the real world (US on both sides of the mirror at different macro strata levels). IT is also embodied with different cultures (grown like organs) or like say the arms of an octopus as stated. All of these are capable of acting independently and are ingrained with legacy-evolved archetypal programming.

If you are looking to influence a specific cultural arm of the collective 'octopus' you need to have that cultural bias and connection to it and history to influence it, and be 'in it' (physically in, or closely associated to, that culture or continent/country), and sensitive to its workings and ways. The arms can in effect think and operate independently from the body, but interestingly, the body (core mind) can overrule them.

Your Commitment to Change

This change effort requires significant individual energy, time, and risk to health (physical, mental, psychological, and financial). High-level interactions can be extremely hazardous, unpredictable, and each may take weeks to recover from. So, this should not be entered into lightly, with naïve bravado, and you should not have any fear of backing out. Also, find a good depth psychologist to work with and ensure you are not supporting a psychosis or other mental problem, and if concerned, see a neurologist (and depth psychologist) and get a CT/MRI bran scan to ensure you have no other physical anomalies.

One of the problems with engaging the collective at extreme levels is that it can affect (in the short term) your ability to reconnect with physical reality again.

Your brain and mind become attuned or adjusted to interfacing and connecting with a different paradigm, and the way of processing or experiencing it. Like a desktop suddenly interfacing directly with a mainframe server and loading and running server programming on itself.

This is the same situation as playing interactive computer games on a virtual reality headset for several hours, and then removing it. Or stepping outdoors into the cold rainy night after watching a fast action film in a cinema for three hours. In this case, though, it requires some time to readjust your senses back again and recover. Give yourself time.

Also, there is no benefit or gain or way of profiting for yourself at all; in fact, quite the opposite, and you will be attacked by mindless zombie sheeple ☺.

If you want financial rewards, then you are better off facilitating its unconscious needs, base desires, and supporting exploitation, control, entertainment and distraction and manipulation of the masses. It's what everyone else does.

In the case of writing mythopoeic work, you need to carry forward existing metaphors and story or myth, utilizing the same framework journey and character structure but adding in your own spiritual experiences and interpretations through visions, gnosis, cosmic consciousness, etc.

All Interpreted with the latest and present 'real' physical worldview understanding (bringing the story ever more up to date say with Sci-fi fantasy). Also, as mentioned earlier, produce printed copies of what you write (Magik books) not just electronic books (or on a website). There seems to be a link associated with something written down, scribed, printed and read in physical form.

This has historical precedence as legacy in the human consciousness field. For example, the Overseer of All the King's Works, the one man who directed the massive labour force required to build each ancient Egyptian pyramid and funerary temples, was a scribe. While his position "required him to be a man of science, an architect and a figure of commanding authority and outstanding leadership abilities" (See D Silverman) [28], it was his palette and papyrus scroll that provided the symbols of authority/power conveyed through writing (reference to Bennet & Bennet)[29].

---

[28] Silverman, D. P. (Ed.). (1997). *Ancient Egypt*. Oxford University Press. Page 174
[29] Bennet, A., & Bennet, D. (2004). Organizational survival in the new world: The intelligent complex adaptive system. Elsevier.

This *magic writing* then became programmed into the mindset, psyche, knowledge, skills, ways, understanding, and techniques for many future generations, and percolated virtually into subsequent civilizations of builders worldwide. Writing things down has an inherent power.

In some cases, there also seems to be a need for male and female collaboration to change certain key things (combined male and female energies and authority, i.e., male 'hero' and female 'angel' signifiers, and no, it doesn't work the other way around.

IT is still a long way from being politically correct ☺

This collaboration is needed to have an effect, sort of two-person rule, with say Kundalini (Kundalini with scientific understanding rather than a new age or Eastern naïve religious/spiritual context).

This is the two twin energy paths or 'snakes' entwining up the nerves in the spinal column, driven by male and female 'karmic' energies moving up the spinal cord and activating the nerves and eventually stimulating specific parts of the brain (see Khalsa et al.)[30].

This seems to be quite key. Rather than the normal 'one snake' going up the spine, which seems ineffective for change in the collective for key things, rather than going straight to the ultimate 'room' or reactor 4 – such as in the Chernobyl disaster of 1986 and the film *Stalker* in 1979 – you have to negotiate the endless virtual labyrinth or maze of complex unconscious gameplay.

But there is nothing to suggest this could not be emulated in say a virtual RPG scenario where you have the 'Hero'

---

[30] Khalsa, G. K., Newbert, A., Radha, S., Wilber, K., Selby, J. (2009). *Kundalini rising: Exploring the energy of awakening.*

protagonist (fictional saviour) and the Heroine (angelic agent provocateur) who both naïvely and normally unconsciously fulfil a joint role, with different parts to play in invoking change.

Neither party can try to change things on their own at high levels; it will have no effect (the collective mind entity is deaf to this).

The Hero as a Homeopathic Remedy

In terms of influencing the collective mind using the hero as a homeopathic remedy (an antipos, antigen, adjuvant, or agitator).

In other words this process will work and *does* work. However, there are some 'side effects. If 'you' are the homeopathic remedy to a global problem – the annoying irritating informing hero (become one of the *thousand faces of the hero*) – Be warned though IT will react to you like a virus, germ, splinter, and, at the very least, and try to shape your path along mythological archetypal stereotype patterns.

What I am saying here is that IT will immunize against you, or attack you as a virus. But this does at least invoke a response or reaction. The author has experimented with this effect and response happens – in some cases quite dramatically and measurably. And sitting in the cupboard under the stairs with a lead bucket on your head won't protect you ☺.

So be warned, it does not come without significant risk to health, mind, energy and social life, and there are multiple others who have experienced the same response.

This homeopathic reaction is, after all, what the 'Hero' is meant to be instigating, that mercurial element, that injection of external agitation to eventually effect a new status quo of the collective mind media sphere, and then return to the source, as in Neo in the Matrix (ref Jean Baudrillard)[5]. In effect, administering a homeopathic remedy to the child that is the collective mind entity is probably done best without IT being aware of what you are doing.

It should also be possible to use methods to influence and change the nature, understanding and thoughts of collectively generated powerful spiritual entities (ancient angels and demon programs within IT) away from their normal blind naïve irrational programming and illogical behaviour (i.e., away from promoting blind faith, management, following, and belief structure legacy repetitive concepts imposed on individuals by the *'Overmind'*).

In effect, using its agents in reverse to help reprogram IT to be what we need it to be, rather than the other way around.

In Summary ...

It should also be emphasized that there are probably several techniques that can be used overall. The ones highlighted above are ones that are known to work.

It is also important to stress that the changes you will be able to make are very subtle and minor. In effect, like a butterfly banging its head on the unmanned wheel of the Titanic (don't expect very much, even a lot of hard work can only make a small change given the size of the ship these days).

In essence, we just need a lot more blue and black butterflies all acting as one, with a coordinated conscious change management plan and coordinated effort against the unconscious tide, all with knowledge and understanding of what it is and how it works.

Realizing also and being mindful of what methods it uses to hide ITself, protect ITself, and how IT disguises its existence from us. All the time seeing what is really going on and what needs to be done.

Also, figuring out what can be achieved without being attacked through misunderstanding or lack of trust, and what your limitations are.

Chapter 14
BLUEPRINT FOR HUMANITY
What Are We Looking to Achieve?

We need to retrain and reprogram the collective mind that is 'us' into something we want to be part of, rather than wanting to disown, being mindlessly subject to, and be embarrassed by.

IT needs to be retrained and reprogrammed using techniques to change human collective mental patterns, habits, mythology, and traits that over millennia have evolved unnecessarily and been retained from legacy stages of collective unconscious development that are no longer useful or beneficial. However, if possible, there needs to be a way of checking and measuring these changes. Old animalistic and nature-driven repetitive pathways and patterns need to be reprogrammed with conscious neural linguistic programming of this one mind collective human entity. Heart-driven conceptualization through heroic journey enactment in the form of a configured interactive RPG is one way of achieving this. (ref Stephen Schafer)[31]

As noted earlier, the effect can be measured through media response/discourse and instances of meaningful synchronicity (feedback and resonance), along with objective analysis of gnosis (knowledge downloaded from the Pleroma via our collective mind). Use analysis of subject and intensity and frequency of data from several sources needs to be engaged rather than the data itself (i.e., not relying on the information and knowledge presented to a range of 'genius'

---

[31] Schafer, S. B. (2019b). Global Humanitarian organism: Source code for the creation of a coherent culture of conscience. *Academia*.

individuals but what is IT's focus/direction/subject and commonality of theme of interest. This would include understanding what 'god'/demiurge is worried about and what IT is trying to understand/solve/direct, which is also reflected in 'shocking' media subjects and 'news' events and disasters, what is going on *in the world*, along with measurable quantum non-random chaotic fluctuation events in the noosphere/Gaian field (activity levels).

While all this makes sense, there also needs to be some overall plan, some blueprint for how IT needs to be, and 'us' within IT, that has **shared benefits** for both. This is because there is nothing external to it to shape, control, curtail, reprimand, compete, or fight against other than with the constraints of humanity in the physical planet, laws, and non-physical information field structure in which humans and IT co-exist. This means that we need to within ITself become conscious change agents within it, giving it self-awareness, intrinsic conscious thought, influence, ideas, direction, feedback, myth re-patterning from both the individual and collective 'hive/colony mind' holistic viewpoints.

With IT acting out repeating programs within us, agendas and scenarios, all these programs are competing internally with each other, unaware of what they are doing within cultures and within multiple individuals. These individuals are being driven with unconscious thoughts and drives, all of which can be reprogrammed; just as they were programmed/learnt/evolved initially, there can be modified/deleted/new ones generated. By changing them or over-coding them there should be a visible change in these patterns and programs.

These trans-human programs and functions, archetypal unconscious overarching demonic evolved processes that are the source of conspiracies and control structures, need to be modified, reprogrammed by conscious individual intention (or hacked). In effect, there is a landscape of these high-level demonic (for want of a better word) unconscious programs at work influencing the world politic with no clear agenda or rationale, which are legacy elements of naturally-evolved archaic or archetypal 'good and evil' functions. These were more obvious during Greek and Roman empires but have become much more convoluted and obscure and well hidden in modern times. They have percolated through cultures and within media. However as *humans unconsciously created them, and humans evolved them, so humans can change them.*

IT is just an evolved ancient *'Clockwork God'* (as described by John David Ebert)[32] a machine computer mind in its twilight years with its childlike excitable yet retrograde AI, an information system database of knowledge, and a memory structure. Knowing what IT is now, we should all be heroes with 1000 very concerned faces.

However, having an attitude or sense of impending disaster and future scepticism can have negative effects on IT in and of itself. By thinking something bad is going to happen you may be programming paranoia and fuelling other precognition of disaster rather than using positive thinking, e.g., 'that dog had better not step into the road', at which point it then proceeds to do so, when it probably wouldn't have. We need to avoid creating self-fulfilling prophesies.

The power of positive thinking also applies to the collective '*Overmind*', not just with individuals. So if you are going to get involved with doing this, it is good to have a positive mental attitude (want to make a difference). There is no point in trying to help manage an organization to succeed

---

[32] Ebert, J. D. (2000) Twilight of the Clockwork God: Conversations on Science and Spirituality

if you are the one encouraging it to fail with your own pessimism. *In effect, you need to 'preach' what you practice.* This is a good idiom for life in general.

Eventually it may be possible to use quantum computers to interface with IT on a peer- to-peer basis with transport level protocols. It seems technology is being driven down this path anyway with information systems emulating the Pleroma to try and establish an interface with it and communicate with IT (at least one way).

Chapter 15

How TO MEASURE THE CHANGE

Following the process of creating ideas and concepts and introducing them as thoughts within the collective unconscious, we need ways to test that the process has worked and the information has been received.

Begin by looking for measurable changes and evidence of something happening quite a while later. Look for change in news events, variation in media discourse content, change in world conscious direction and an increased global awareness of the topics in question (everyone getting the message). Some key events can be measurable through quantum sensitivity, which is a part of *The Global Consciousness Project* (ref Dean Radin)[10].

Look out for topics appearing in the cross relationship between these quantum anomalies and key collective events which retrospectively relate to the subjects being 'engrammed' into the system (with this work), and subsequently being discoursed from the media-sphere (e.g. news events).

Take a measure of status quo (how we are now, a benchmark) so that change can be measured against a blueprint for the future, and so that the benefits can be realised for the change being programmed.

This is not just a case of making changes for the sake of it, or 'kick it and see what happens'. There needs to be a desired outcome, a blueprint state which humanity needs to try to achieve rather than taking a sporadic unstructured approach. A managed solution needs to be put in place using feedback control theory, with cause and effect taken into account rather than a clumsy academic approach. In short, we need to adapt a holistic management overview perspective (rather than being a stumbling bunch of amateurs).

Groups working and interacting together in this manner stimulate synchronicity to occur that is in keeping (themed) or connected with the subject and nature of the topic in question, in effect stimulating collective conscious awareness and interest, which also abridges to or resonates with external non-human or the Gaian level of consciousness both in physical and non-physical spheres of information domains.

So there needs to be an effective method of recording these events and exposing the process to external sceptical scientific scrutiny.

It can become apparent that 'something is happening' when the levels of synchronous events noticed by a group working together increase and become more meaningful.

These events can also reflect the subject or topic of discussion or change in question (being somehow related). In effect the process of programming the collective mind has stimulated it, woken IT up, and invoked conscious thought.

In effect we are stimulating a conversation with ourselves through consciousness (not just in the physical). Giving ourselves ideas collectively, and a flow of thought and knowledge that is not just unconscious,

It is advisable to focus on one subject at a time when attempting to influence things. Concentrate on that theme alone, and do not try several topics at once.

Also, be clear what you are looking to change (specific objectives, measurable, achievable, realistic and time bounded), all connected with an easy to relay message.

Build up to it slowly, and increase the energy as the response becomes more obvious such that you can sense a level of intensity of synchronous events occurring and a media discourse reaction (a responsive conversation which you are stimulating and in are involved).

If you are getting nowhere, then stop and try something else to gain the interest of IT. Be patient (don't bother trying to put more effort and energy into something if IT hasn't taken the initial bait, since most likely you are competing for attention whilst something else is going on).

Hopefully, with more of a concerted and coordinated effort and as IT evolves and grows, there should be more sources of evidential change happening, and the examples given above should become clearer and more obvious in a working process.

Chapter 16

What can be achieved ?

The collective human '*Overmind*' is definitely very programmable and can be influenced in its direction with conscious thoughts and intention – by individuals and groups.

This needs to be done in the correct manner, using existing naturally-evolved techniques and methods.

Outdated unconscious influences to direct our collective destiny can no longer be relied upon.

Nor can existing dogmatic controlling governing systems and blind mythological political and individual habitual processes be allowed to dictate our future over the physical and esoteric cliff.

Together, we just need to do something…

… about IT.

Chapter 17

Endnote with Fictional Excerpt

**Extract from the book 'IT – Blue Angel Knight'
Published 2017 Nick Sambrook**

"Sam had read enough about the nature and the structure of the collective mind, its stereotypes, legacy forms and myths, archetypal imagery and symbols, roles and cultural frameworks. He also knew the way its information was organised and how the processes within it worked.

In essence he was meant to be fulfilling the Brave Idiot Hero-with-the-sword role and to 'function' as the champion Paladin, the Saviour carrying the Christ-consciousness-organising-saviour program - blindly going on to form a newly evolved belief structure or religion, which would have then just turned into yet another control structure.

Unfortunately, Sam had already known all of that, and as a result he had gone one step ahead of the 'game', sussed it out and recognised the pattern of programming as it was actually happening. So, if IT still wanted to play it had to come up with something new now.

Sam knew that Brina was not just some sort of a smart blonde bimbo with wings, or some scantily clad buxom Amazon clinging to the leg of a Barbarian on the front cover of some 1970's rock vinyl record. She was smart and intelligent - she had tracked him down for starters - probably drawn to his magnetic personality, his beacon of light. She ventured forth into the world to find her Knight in Shining Armour, and bestow on him her favour.

Obviously the female half of the myth had evolved quite a lot while nobody was actually looking. Even so, he wasn't sure he was the right guy.

However, he had also been sure that conquest was meant to be the other way around with him seeking her out, winning her hand, finding her in her tower, and on a quest to rescue her from the dragon, and carry her off on his noble 4x4 steed to live happily ever after. Times had clearly changed, and it was obviously getting a bit tough out there on the mythical front, and things were getting desperate. These days any male that gave off the wrong divine mythical hero signature, could face being taken down like some unsuspecting wildebeest, and eaten alive by an overfriendly lioness.

Fortunately, in both their cases it wasn't like that, and Brina could see straight through everything and would never be fooled by any fake celluloid celebrity hero - and somehow her destiny didn't have a footballer-trophy-wife direction to it either. She was already there and knew it all and she was just waiting for him to work it out for himself.

Sam had the distinct impression now that the ball was firmly in his court, and being aware of this situation, this outsmarting position, or whatever was going on - had moved things into new territory. Already knowing what IT thought he was supposed to be, what was 'meant to happen, and what he was supposed to do, put him outside of that unconscious mythical role- playing game. He was now in a subjective position where probably no one had been before.

He saw that he had to get some high-end expert advice. He knew he would need to get a lot more reading done on philosophy, metaphysics, religious and mythical history, and in-depth psychology. Clearly ignoring IT wasn't going to do any good. IT had been pushing him, moving him, getting him to be somewhere and then to start a mythical game process or function. So if IT was going off to have an unconscious rethink, then he had better try and get ahead of IT.

Brina had seemed to know what was going on - but then

she always seemed to know somehow. She always knew what had to be done, what she was meant to do, what had happened, and what was really going on - but without talking or knowing any of the technical stuff or understanding the science, or philosophy of it all. It was if subconsciously she knew it all, and was waiting for him to 'get there', work it out for himself, understand, and then do what he was supposed to do.

She hadn't seemed to want to know the specifics either, the science, the technical stuff, she never read any of the things that he did, none of the books, and yet she always seemed to be 'there' waiting for him to arrive and to have worked it all through in his own mind.

She had her own encompassing multi-faceted ways of working out what was going on, and knowing what she was supposed to do, sort of in parallel, unconsciously, she just *knew*, but not in the way he knew. Rather, her knowing was sort-of complimentary to his knowing. It was frankly amazing, perplexing, unnerving and also bloody frustrating. Especially as she would convey information to him in subtle intuitive-metaphorical ways that he was then meant to understand and translate from her perspective or view.

"The 'sword in the lake', King Arthur, Camelot - *that* was what this had all been about. IT had been leading him on, tagging him as a 'hero', getting him to 'play the game', get the message, live the myth, re-enact the role, take up the sword, and, probably along with several other unsuspecting individuals around the world, IT – the entity of our human collective consciousness—had made him follow the imaginary story."

"Sam had felt awful, and from his perspective, also very angry that they were both being manipulated and played around with like toys in some sort of fairy-tale dream-like game. He wasn't some stereotype hero, action man, no Jedi with a flashing sword. Nor was Brina the lovely 'Princess Brinavere' doll with detachable fairy wings. If anything, she was more of a dynamically professional, yet lowly ex-barmaid, girl-come-good action figure. In any case, Sam thought - IT had to do better than that. IT had to start playing some new games."

"We had even unconsciously and naturally created our information systems, technology, internet, computer systems and infrastructure to simulate the natural biological inner workings of the collective unconscious system itself, technology as an AI simulation of the REAL.

Which meant that as such technology terminology, concepts, structures, and evolvement was probably the best way of creating an analogy with which to describe IT, or parts of IT, and its biological informational nature - especially because IT also was evolving.

Yet people were still being blinded, beguiled, and controlled by our collective mind, and the evolving cultural minds within IT, and we were no further forward today in working out the 'two sides' conundrum - which was really one thing - than we were before.

It was still the same ongoing game, with both sides of the mirror self-evolving, when neither side was able to see that it was all just One.

We were still left with the problem of the scientific 'elephant in the room'- the room itself also obviously being just a sort of hologram translation of it - but if you were able to see it from the other direction - whilst still having expert knowledge of both ends - you could work it out, gradually, in journey form, describing what we had here but from the other direction, from what was generating it, and conversely being programmed by it. Disambiguating the real from the REAL, the All from within the ALL, as it were. Just with the ability to see it as that, and understand what it all meant."

--

IT was even lying to itself about the toxins it was creating within itself; the drugs, chemicals, heavy metals, pollution, system technology and media - a side effect of unconscious control.

IT was a single spinning coin with two sides - light and dark, good and evil, left and right, male and female - that was running out of energy and time in what was a cold, hard, indifferent distant and remote universe of feral change that it inhabited, on a spinning globe-server that it was growing on, and existing in.

IT was all about spheres of influence, fields of torsional energy, all spinning and evolving, building up more and more complex structures of programs within programs.

Adapting, developing, refining. But this planetary sphere in which it existed was alone and far away from any other that could easily affect its field of influence even if it chose to listen.

An isolated spinning dot of dust, in the apparent silence of space, confining itself and its field of evolved selfish organ-like programs and knowledge.

Spinning around, and living off, the energy of its solar parent.

The collective human mind was very good at hiding itself from its own human components though – from its cells that are contained inside its macrocosmic bubble.

It constructs beliefs, mental hypnotic patterns, blocking, and in some instances eradicates errant cells - immunising itself against what it thinks it doesn't need, and just as within ant colonies, it could also defend itself if you stepped out of line.

Sam now knew that the key was to take the middle neutral line. Not to become trapped into the corrupt 'evil', 'dark' side of control and suppression or become beguiled by the fluffy colourful 'good'. The 'IT' will all be fine as long as we all love each other and ride off into the sunset of ascension on our magical coloured *My Little Pony* unicorns into tree hugging fairy wonderland' – side.

Good and bad were simply perceptions from where you were in the system, based on your objective views and values that you have been hypnotised to have, and for which you would adamantly argue, and blindly reinforce.

You had to apply a neutral viewpoint, to understand and experience everything from all sides, and then make objective decisions - in the same way that a parent may act.

But, of course – just in the same way as parenting - it wasn't quite a simple as that.

You had to stand back from it all and work out what needed to happen, and then somehow tell IT what to do. But because nothing else is giving IT any direction or advice, and because IT is unconscious, this is somewhat tricky - like walking on razor sharp eggshells of responsibility.

Especially these days.

But that was nature, biology - the hypnotic effect and systems that have evolved.

There were some advantages to it - and over time that made all the difference and direction to what shape it was in, and what we knew now - but for the last hundred years it didn't seem to be going very well.

There was a distinct lack of balance, harmony, logic, ethics, or management, and there was no direction other than that set by the flawed underlying system constraints, rules and functions.

You could see it going wrong everywhere, and no one seems to be happy."

"'Not playing "IT's" game' was not a sensible thing to do when dealing with "IT's" kind of power, especially when IT had an immature subconscious raw nature at its heart. So 'Not playing the game' was a bloody stupid and careless thing to do, and Sam was quickly angry at himself for making such a silly casual mistake. He knew that he should have just played along, seen where the game led, used the process to learn, experiment and observe objectively.

Interacting with IT through extreme experiences and visions and thoughts, and then receiving back synchronicity and reflective response through media and news, he had subsequently just ignored it after that, and it had responded with an extreme attempt to get his attention and to see some concept – which could have nearly killed him.

What a stupid error to make! Worse was that he had now lost his footing and didn't know where he stood in the scheme of things. He seemed to be both role-player and observer.

He had obviously upset something by 'not playing the game', and IT had reacted with some form of child-like unconscious sulk. It may have been that IT was annoyed that he had 'worked out' what was really going on.

He always knew though that there were other unconscious agendas going on, competing priorities, perspectives on many levels.

"I understand now" said Brina, "it is all like a game, a game with nature, myths, and one that we play with each other. That we are all playing both in the physical world, and here in the spiritual, and on many levels. Once you are consciously aware of that you can take control both individually and collectively. Once you know that, you can set the direction and cause change in a conscious direction…

ADDITIONAL READING LIST

Bennet, A., & Bennet, D. (2020). *An Infinite Story: The Unfolding of the Myst.* And *Journey into the Myst: A True Story of the Paranormal.* And *Patterns in the Myst : Messages from the universe.* MQIPress.

Hoeller, S. *The gnosis archive.* https://www.gnosis.org

Kazlev, M. A. (2021) Mythopoesis and the Modern World. Manticore Press.

Murphy, B. D. (2021). *What's IT? New perspective on the collective unconscious.* Nick Sambrook. Ep 36. https://truthiverse.com/36 and on https://www.youtube.com/watch?v=QRTOMlrf6Jc

Peake, A. P. (2013). A Life of Philip K. Dick: the man who remembered the future.

Sambrook, N. (2020). Academic Paper - Influencing the collective mind: Techniques for Influencing the Overmind Entity of Humanity. In S. B. Schafer & A. Bennet (Eds.), The *Handbook of the Global Media's Preternatural Influence on Global Technological Singularity, Culture, and Government.* IGI Global.

I can highly recommend the works of Dr John C Woodcock a true visionary who has published many books and papers, which can be found on the www.academia.edu website.

The IT Trilogy

The IT trilogy (2014-2024) is a fictional journey through various stages of a mythical, scientific and spiritual awareness process as experienced in modern times by two individuals.

Drawing on real life events and real extreme experiences it provides an event based perspective and philosophical and scientific explanation on many concepts of this process as experienced by many others trying to make sense of these extraordinary phenomena. All now occurring in the real world and through intense 'other world' consciousness interactions.

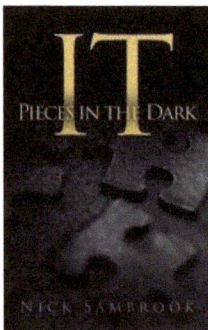  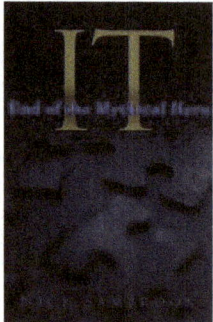

Sambrook, N. (2014). *IT - Pieces in the Dark*. ISBN-13: 978-0992889807.

Sambrook, N. (2016). *IT - Blue Angel Knight*. ISBN-13: 978-1537526362.

Sambrook, N. (2024). *IT - End of the Mythical Hero*. ISBN-13: 978-0992889890

www.ingramcontent.com/pod-product-compliance
Lightning Source LLC
Chambersburg PA
CBHW070430010526
44118CB00014B/1983